DAY TRADING:

2 Books In 1

The Ultimate Trading Guide for Beginners. Learn
the Importance of Stock Market Moves and Swing
Trading to Create Wealth
and Make A Profit Online

By **James N. Miles**

DAY TRADING:

The strategy Bible to Invest in
Leveraging Options, Stocks, Forex,
and Making the Most of Market Swings.
The Ultimate Guide for Beginning Traders to
Build a Profitable Passive Income (Part 1)

By **James N. Miles**

Table of Contents

CHAPTER 1: HISTORY OF DAY TRADING 8

CHAPTER 2: DAY TRADING FOR BEGINNERS 22

KEY TIPS FOR BEGINNERS 23

WHAT CAN MAKE DAY TRADING DIFFICULT 26

DECIDE WHEN TO SELL... 29

HOW TO REDUCE LOSSES DURING DAY TRADING 31

GERMANE DAY TRADING STRATEGIES 32

BIGGEST MISTAKES TO AVOID WHILE DAY TRADING 34

CHAPTER 3: MORE TIPS FOR BEGINNERS ON DAY
TRADING 46

TOOLS FOR DAY TRADING BEGINNERS 48

BEST TIMES FOR DAY TRADING 50

MORE TIPS ON MANAGING YOUR DAY TRADING RISK 52

PRACTICING STRATEGIES FOR DAY TRADING BEGINNERS.......... 53

THE WORD FOR DAY TRADING BEGINNERS 55

CHAPTER 4: DAY TRADING STRATEGIES A TO Z 57

FOREX DAY TRADING SYSTEMS... 60

CHAPTER 5: DAY TRADING SIGNALS 73

CHAPTER 6 DAY TRADING FOREX 78

DO'S AND DON'T'S IN FOREX TRADING................................. 83

THE FINAL VERDICT... 91

CHAPTER 7: HOW TO START DAY TRADING WITH $500 .93

DAY TRADING:

The strategy Bible to Invest in
Leveraging Options, Stocks, Forex,
and Making the Most of Market Swings.
The Ultimate Guide for Beginning Traders to
Build a Profitable Passive Income (Part 2)

By **James N. Miles**

Table of Contents

CHAPTER 8: DAY TRADING FOR A LIVING 107

STEP BY STEP INSTRUCTIONS TO MAKE A LIVING **112**

CHAPTER 9: DAY TRADING FOR DUMMIES 140

WHY DAY TRADING?..**123**

CHAPTER 10: GUIDE TO CRYPTO TRADING 130

CHAPTER 11: AVERAGE INCOME OF A DAY TRADER 144

A DAY TRADING STRATEGY IN REAL LIFE **154**

THE AMOUNT MONEY STOCK DAY TRADERS MAKE - FINAL WORD
....**157**

CHAPTER 12: DAY TRADING ACADEMIES 160

CHAPTER 13: DAY TRADING WEBSITES 164

CHAPTER 14: DAY TRADING DO'S AND DON'T'S..................182

CHAPTER 1:

HISTORY OF DAY TRADING

History of Day Trading

In present-day times, we underestimate day trading. It sounds good to us that somebody can purchase a stock and sell it around the same time.

Be that as it may, day trading is a moderately new idea. The historical backdrop of day trading has experienced numerous twists and turns throughout the years, yet it has never been more conspicuous than it is today.

When did the day trading start? To what extent has day trading existed? Today, we're going to let you know all that you have to think about the historical backdrop of day trading.

Day Trading Started with the Ticker Tape

Day trading can be followed right back to 1867. As opposed to what numerous individuals accept, day trading didn't develop with the ascent of PCs or the web. It follows its history back to even before electricity.

Before the web and other worldwide correspondence stages were created, representatives would attempt to live near the New York Stock Exchange, as it implied they were getting an enduring inventory of ticker tape with the most exceptional data.

Today, ticker tape alludes to the flood of electronic data gushing over a pennant. In past times, it was a solid sheet of paper. Merchants would utilize ticker tape to make educated choices on financial exchange developments for the day, taking into account a few specialists to take an interest in day trading.

All through the early history of securities exchanges, singular brokers didn't have direct access to business sectors. All requests were set through an agent. Merchants utilized data gathered off the ticker tape.

This type of trading was regular all through the beginning of securities exchanges. Be that as it may, the hindrances to passage implied day trading was not prevalent among the overall public.

A Communication Network is Created

In 1971, the spread of financial exchange data around the globe turned out to be more productive than at any time in recent memory. That year, the National Association of Securities Dealers made an electronic correspondence arrange (ECN). That ECN was known as the National Association of Securities Dealers Automated Quotation System. Today, we know it as the NASDAQ.

An ECN is characterized as any PC framework that encourages money related items exchanges outside of stock trades. This opened financial transactions and contributing to singular speculators – not merely merchants.

All of a sudden, a wide range of trading – including day trading – was increasingly available to the average man. It was, as yet, far away from turning into a well known or basic movement among small-time, singular financial specialists.

Fixed Commission Exchanges Are Abolished

For the whole early history of American financial exchanges (180 years), there were fixed rates on transactions. Markets had set costs on all trades, which implied that representatives couldn't rival different merchants on price

In 1975, it changed –financial exchange world until the end of time. That year, the Securities and Exchange Commission (SEC) set up rules abolishing fixed commissions.

That implied, without precedent for a long time, trading expenses on financial exchanges were chosen by showcase rivalry – which appears as though an appropriate method to select things identified with the securities exchange. Because of these changes, Charles Schwab and other firms started enabling clients to exchange stocks at limited commission rates, denoting the start of the rebate specialist time. Dealers began to contend with each other by offering lower and lower prices. These dealers started to advance and try different things with new trading frameworks that made the procedure increasingly productive. Indeed, trading stocks turned out to be a lot simpler for singular speculators. Not exclusively might they be able to get to securities exchanges completely, yet they could do it at a lower cost from a developing number of representatives, vast numbers of which emerged during this time-span to address request.

ECNs Make Trading Easier for the Mediocre Investor

Various Electronic Communication Networks (ECNs) would show up over the coming years, including understood names like Instinet (which still exists right up 'til the present time, and was established before NASDAQ, in 1969).

These ECNs emerged to address the interest of speculators. Driven by another time of focused commission rates, ECNs had the option to serve a developing scope of customers. ECNs had an essential job in the market: they were robotized frameworks that coordinated the purchase and sale orders for protections.

All the more critically, ECNs associated singular dealers with major financiers, enabling both to purchase/sell protections from the other without using an agent. This drove expenses down much further, making day trading considerably easier.

During this time, ECNs like Instinet, SelectNet, and NYSE Arca would all get noticeable in the business.

Instinet is the best-known and was generally utilized all through the 1970s, 80s, and 90s for NASDAQ exchanges. Some portion of its prominence was that people and small firms could likewise use it.

SelectNet, then again, was utilized principally by showcase producers. Right up until today, it doesn't require prompt request execution. It's used to assist speculators with trading with explicit market creators.

NYSE Arca was an ECN that rise out of a mix of the NYSE and Archipelago, an early ECN from 1996. It encourages electronic stock trading on significant US trades – like NYSE as well as NASDAQ.

In October 1987, the financial exchange crashed, uncovering a central issue with how markets worked for singular speculators.

What was that issue? In this time, most exchanges were directed via telephone. At the point when the financial market crashed, specialists had a simple method for staying away from the issue: they quit answering their phones. Financial specialists would call to urgently attempt to sell their stocks, just to be overlooked.

The SEC saw this imperfection and presented an elective framework called Small Order Entry System (SOES). This framework gave requests of 1,000 offers or less a priority over more significant demands.

This change secured singular, small financial specialists in the business sectors. Like the entirety of different changes referenced above, it expelled one more boundary to a section between singular speculators and the economic exchange, encouraging day trading much further.

The Dot Com Craze of 1997 Shows Another Issue with Markets

At the point when you enable a great many individual speculators to put resources into the securities exchange effortlessly, it uncovers another essential market issue: it acquaints mass brain science with the financial transaction at a level never recently observed.

This was best seen in 1997 when the website furor filled hypothesis in innovation stocks. The web was spreading to family units over the created world, and individuals were purchasing any shares identified with the internet. During this timeframe, online merchants like E-Trade propelled administrations that made it considerably simpler for speculators to contribute. E-Trade turned out to be exceptionally outstanding for enabling individual financial specialists to take an interest in IPOs effortlessly.

On account of the web, small merchants currently had direct access to value cites, trading exercises, and other relevant market data. This made everything fair for everybody. Some enormous agents even contended that the market supported small dealers because these merchants could exploit SOES (the framework that gave small brokers priority over more prominent dealers).

The universe of tech stocks was blasting, and day trading was rapidly turning into a "thing" individuals did. It wasn't unheard of for a typical financial specialist with little market understanding to rake in some serious cash on the securities exchange by getting one stock toward the beginning of the day and afterward selling it toward the evening at 400% edge rates. Somewhere within the range of 1997 and 2000, the NASDAQ detonated with development, ascending from 1200 to 5000.

Day Trading Continued to Expand in 1999

By 1999, day trading had become an out and out wonder.

Notwithstanding, in contrast with day trading today, there weren't the same number of informal investors as you're most likely reasoning. It was a unique little something that many individuals heard individuals did – yet few "normal" individuals took an interest.

As a demonstration of that reality, Arthur Levitt, Chairman of the SEC, affirmed before Congress in 1999 that the number of informal investors was around 7,000.

In the examination, Mr. Levitt evaluated that there were around 5 million web clients bought into online specialists.

In the same way as other things individuals didn't comprehend, day trading became dreaded and questioned. During this timeframe, day trading had a negative undertone. The pessimistic demeanor towards day trading finished in a shooting binge at an Atlanta day trading office, where Mark Barton killed

12 individuals and injured 13 others after losing an expected $105,000 in day trading over a multi-month time frame.

The Barton episode persuaded numerous individuals that day trading was so upsetting it could convince a generally normal man to commit mass homicide.

Day trading as a calling endured another shot when, two weeks after the Barton shootings, the North American Securities Administrators Association released a report saying that 7 out of 10 informal investors lose everything. They don't merely lose cash by and large – they lose all that they've contributed.

2000: The SOES Advantage is Eliminated

Before 2000, probably the most significant bit of leeway informal investors had was SOES, the framework that guaranteed that exchanges under 1,000 were tended to before transactions more than 1,000, giving a bit of space to smaller merchants. The structure was intended to urge singular financial specialists to enter the market, yet it, in the long run, prompted informal investors having an out of line benefits.

In 2000, SOES was changed. The most significant change was that it disposed of the points of interest for informal investors.

The Dot Com Bubble Bursts

The changing of the SOES was one disheartening unforeseen development for informal investors. Not long after the SOES was changed, another colossal change occurred: the website bubble burst.

Accordingly, numerous informal investors failed or lost a lot of their money. Many were frightened off from the calling and looked for new vocations. The prime of being a casual investor had all the earmarks of being finished.

This marked the finish of an extraordinary time of day trading. Before the website air pocket collapsed, day trading was seen as the Wild West. Informal investors were hoping to make a quick buck. Speculators were centered around pump and dump plans. Guidelines were restricted.

After the website bubble burst, in any case, day trading would turn out to be substantially more like customary contributing – it was something healthy financial specialists could without much of a stretch take an interest in.

Day Trading during the 2000s

The website air pocket's end denoted the finish of one time of day trading. However, it was the beginning of another period of day trading. Rather than "easy money scams" and untamed outskirts style trading, day trading during the 2000s began to have a progressively proficient frame of mind.

HowStuffWorks.com refers to the US Department of Labor when it says that there were 320,000 protections, wares, and money related help operators in 2006 over the United States, and that number incorporates informal investors. By and by, we don't have a particular breakdown of the number of casual investors.

As a theory, HowStuffWorks.com gauges that 5% to 10% of expert money related assistance specialists are informal investors, which would mean 16,000 to 32,000 people revealed their day trading income to the US Department of Labor in 2006. In any case, all outnumber of informal investors is a lot higher, as a beginner and low maintenance casual investors "may number in the millions" (Source).

Forex Trading during the 2000s

Trading remote monetary standards are nearly as old as the development itself. Present-day forex trading comes substantially later and just showed up after the finish of the Bretton Woods framework during the 1970s. The finish of the Bretton Woods framework implied that the US dollar was never again pegged to the cost of gold. The period of fixed trade rates was finished, and it was another time of fluctuating trade rates.

Why am I revealing to you this in an article about the history of day trading?

Forex and day trading go inseparably. As foreign trade (forex) trading turned out to be increasingly standard, so too did day trading.

TradingAcademy.com reports that in 1980, outside trade exchanges meant $70 billion per day in absolute worth. By 2003, that number had expanded to $2.4 trillion per day.

Most forex brokers don't take an interest in day trading. Money advertises seldom change generally enough to make a considerable benefit through day trading. Numerous dealers take an interest in present moment forex exchanges, or use forex as one piece of their day trading business.

What would be an ideal next step?

Today, day trading stays a famous action among both expert financial specialists and novices. A few people will reveal to you day trading is an unsafe action, while others will persuade you that it's a simple method to make easy money. The truth is someplace in the middle, and it, to a great extent, relies upon your ability as an individual speculator.

Your aptitude as an informal investor is firmly connected to your expertise as a general speculator. It requires brilliant research and systematic abilities –

and a thoughtful piece of karma. Present-day markets are uneven. However, they likewise move quick. Regardless of whether you're looking at a brief period or a multi-month time frame, trading in the course of the most recent couple of years has been a rough street.

The present informal investors utilize current research devices and calculations with an end goal to time the market. Types of day trading – like paired choices trading and forex trading – have gotten synonymous with "trick" in the online world, as urgent individuals search for any approach to make a quick buck on the web.

CHAPTER 2:

DAY TRADING FOR BEGINNERS

Day trading is the process of buying and selling a financial instrument across the course of a day on the same day or even multiple times. It can be a profitable game to take advantage of small price moves— when it is played correctly.

But for newbies and anyone who does not pursue a well-thought-out approach, it can be a dangerous game. However, not all brokers are suited to day traders' high volume of trades. Nevertheless, some brokers are designed for the day trader.

Digital brokers on our list, including Tradestation, TD Ameritrade, and Interactive

Brokers, have qualified and specialized platform models offering real-time streaming offers, sophisticated charting software, and the ability to enter and change multiple orders quickly.

Look at some general day trading concepts and then determine when to buy and sell specific day trading strategies, simple charts, and trends, and how to minimize losses.

Key Tips for beginners

1. INFORMATION IS POWER; In addition to knowledge of basic trading techniques, day traders need to keep up with the latest stock market news and information impacting stocks— interest rate forecasts from the Fed, economic outlook, etc. Do your studies like that. Make a wish list of shares you want to trade and keep you up-to-date on selected companies as well as general markets. Check news from the industry and visit reputable financial websites.

2. SET ASIDE FUNDS; evaluate how much capital you are willing to risk for each company. Most successful day traders lose their account from less than 1 percent to 2 percent per trade.

If you get a trading account of $40,000 and are willing to risk 0.5% of your money on each deal, the maximum loss is $200 (0.005 x $40,000) per exchange. Set aside a surplus amount of money that you can trade with and are willing to lose. Note, it might or might not happen.

3. SET ASIDE A GOOD TIME; it takes some time to exchange on day training. Which is why it's called day trading; in reality, you will have to give up most of your day. If you have little spare time, don't do it. The process requires a trader to monitor stocks and spot advantages that can happen during trading hours at any time. It's essential to move quickly.

4. BEGIN SMALL; As a beginner, concentrate during a session on a total of one or two stocks. With just a few stocks, it's easier to track and find opportunities.

Recently, the ability to trade fractional shares has become increasingly common, so you can assign different, smaller dollar values that you want to invest. This means if you're selling Apple stock at $250 and want to buy just $50 worth, most brokers would now let you get one-fifth of a share.

5. AVOID PENNY STOCKS; but stay away from penny stocks, you're just looking for deals and low prices. Such stocks are often illiquid, and there are often grim chances of reaching a jackpot. Most shares traded under $5 a share are de-listed from major stock exchanges and are only over-the-counter (OTC) tradable. Stay clear of these unless you see a real chance and have done your research.

6. TIME THOSE TRADES; most investors and traders position orders start executing as soon as the morning markets open, which leads to price volatility. A professional player will identify trends and choose to make profits accordingly. But for newbies, it may be best to read the market for the first 15 to 20 minutes without making any moves. The mid hours are typically less unpredictable and then moved toward the closing bell starts to pick up again. Although the peak hour offers opportunities, avoiding them at first is easier for beginners.

7. CUT LOSSES WITH LIMIT ORDERS; decide what kind of orders you are going to use to join and leave companies. Are you going to use business orders or restrict orders? It is executed at the best price at the time that you put a market order— thus, no-cost guarantee. Whereas, a limit order guarantees the cost, but not the output. Limit orders help you trade more efficiently by setting your value (not impossible but executable) for both buying and selling. More sophisticated and seasoned day traders can also use strategies with options to hedge their bets.

8. BE REALISTIC ABOUT EARNINGS; to be successful, a plan doesn't have to win all the time. Many traders win just 50% to 60% of the trades. They make so much on their winners, however, then on their losers. Ensure that the risk for each exchange is restricted to a particular account percentage and that methods of entry and exit are clearly defined and written down.

9. KEEP COOL; often, the emotions are checked by stock markets. You need to learn to keep covetousness, optimism, and apprehension at bay as a day trader. Decisions should be governed by reason rather than emotion.

10. STICK TO THE PLAN; Successful traders need to move quickly, though they don't need to think fast. What's the reason? Because in advance, they have established a trading strategy, along with the discipline to stick to that strategy. Instead of trying to chase money, it is essential to follow the formula carefully.

Don't let your feelings get your best and give up your plan. There is a mantra among day traders: "Planning your trade and selling your plan." Let's look at some of the causes why day trading can be so challenging before we delve into some of the ins and outs of day trading.

What Can Make Day Trading Difficult

Trading on a day takes experience and know-how, and there are a variety of factors that can complicate the process.

Next, know that you're up against experts whose jobs have to do with trading. Such people have access to the industry's best technologies and networks, so they are set up to thrive even if they fail eventually. This means more money for them if you jump on the bandwagon.

And you're going to have to pay taxes at the marginal rate on any short-term gains—or any assets you keep for a year or less. The one downside is that the losses offset any gains.

You may be prone to emotional and cognitive biases as an individual investor. Professional traders can tend to cut these out of their trading strategies, but it appears to be a different story when it's your investments involved.

DECIDING WHEN AND WHAT TO BUY; Day traders actually make money by manipulating tiny price fluctuations in individual assets (stocks, currencies, futures, as well as options), typically using lots of capital to do just that. When deciding what to concentrate on — in a stock, say— a traditional day trader is searching for three things: liquidity: you can get in and out of stock at a reasonable price.

Tight spreads, for example, or the difference between a stock's bid and demand price, or low slippage or the disparity between a trade's expected price and the actual price.

Volatility: Volatility is purely a function of the daily price range that is expected— the range in which a day trader works. The volatility is more gain or disadvantage.

Trade volume: This is a calculation of how many times a stock is bought and sold over a given period— most commonly known as the daily average rate of trade.

A high volume shows a lot of attention in a stock. The change in the price of a stock is often an indicator of a price jump, whether upwards or downwards. When you know what kind of stocks (or other assets) that you are looking for, you'll need to learn how to recognize entry points — that's when you're going to invest. Tools you can use to do it include:

REAL-TIME NEWS SERVICES: News moves markets, so subscribing to services that tell you when market-driven news comes out is essential.

ECN / LEVEL 2 QUOTES: ECNs or electronic communications networks are software-based systems that show the best bid available and demand quotes by multiple market participants and afterward match and implement orders automatically. Level 2 is a subscription-based service that gives real-time entry to the NASDAQ order book consisting of market makers' price quotes reporting through NASDAQ as well as OTC Bulletin Board protection. These will give you necessary insights into the real-time execution of orders

CHARTS OF INTRADAY CANDLESTICKS: candlesticks provide a direct price action analysis. Much information on these later on.

Identify the circumstances in which you will reach a position and write them down. "Buy uptrend" is not very precise. Something like this is far more accurate and also testable: "Buy on the two-minute graph in the first two hours of trading day when price breaks above the upper trend of a triangle pattern, where an uptrend followed the triangle (at least one higher swing highs and lower swing low before the triangle was formed). Once you have a set of entry rules, search through more charts to see if those conditions are created every day (assuming you want daily trade) and, more often than not, make a price move in the expected direction. If so, for a plan, you have a possible entry point. Then you will have to decide how to exit and sell specific trades.

Decide when to sell

There are several ways to leave a winning position, including trailing stops and benefit targets. The most popular exit strategy is revenue goals, making a profit at a defined rate. Some specific procedures for the price target are:

SCALPING

One of the most common techniques is scalping. This involves selling after a deal is profitable almost immediately. The price target is anything that translates into "you've made money on this deal."

FADING

Fading means shortening stocks following fast upward moves. This is based on the assumption that:

(1) they are overbought,

(2) early buyers are willing to start taking profits, and

(3) current buyers may be frightened.

This technique may be advantageous but risky. The price target here is when buyers begin to re-enter.

DAILY PIVOTS

This strategy involves taking advantage of the daily fluctuations of a stock.

This is done by trying to buy at day's low and sell at day's peak. The price target here is the next indicator of a turnaround.

MOMENTUM

This approach usually involves betting on news releases or spotting significant, high-volume trend movements. On news releases, one form of momentum trader can buy and ride a trend until it shows signs of reversal. The other kind is going to fade the price increase. The price target here is when volume starts to fall.

In most cases, if there is reduced interest in the stock as shown by level 2/ECN and size, you will want to exit an asset. The profit goal should also make it possible to make more profit on winning trades than it is on losing trades. If your stop-loss is $0.05 away from the entry price, it should be more than $0.05 away from your goal.

Specify exactly how you will exit your trades before joining them, just like your entry point. The exit requirements must be sufficiently precise for reproducibility and screening.

How to Reduce Losses during Day Trading

Another technique is to set two stop losses: a physical stop-loss order put at a certain price that fits your tolerance for threat. This is practically the most money you can afford to lose.

A psychological stop-loss at the point of breach of your entry criteria. This means you can automatically leave your place if the trade takes an unexpected turn.

The exit conditions must be sufficiently precise to be testable and repeatable if you choose to exit your trades. Setting a maximum loss per day that you can afford to withstand — both financially and mentally — is also critical. Take the rest of the day off immediately you reach this stage.

Stick to your perimeter and prepare. Tomorrow, after all, is another day for trading.

You can assess if the potential strategy fits within your risk limit once you have defined how you enter trades and where you will place a stop loss. If you are exposed to too much danger in the plan, you need to change the strategy to reduce the risk in some way.

If the strategy falls within the risk limit, testing will start. To locate your entries manually, go through historical charts, and see if your stop loss or goal was reached. In this way, paper trading for at least 50 to 100 trades, indicating if the strategy was successful and meeting your expectations.

Finally, bear in mind that if margin trading—which means you borrow your investment funds from a brokerage firm (and keep in mind that day trading margin requirements are high)—you are much more vulnerable to sharp price movements.

Margin helps to increase the results of trading not only by profit but also by losses if a trade goes against you. Therefore, when trading on the margin day, the use of stop losses is essential.

Now that you know of some of the ins and outs of day trading, let's take a quick look at a number of the main strategies that new day traders can use.

Germane Day Trading Strategies

Once you have mastered a number of the techniques, developed your styles of trading, and set what your end goals are, you can implement a series of strategies to assist you in your quest for profit.

You can use some standard techniques here. Although some of these have been listed above, it's worth going back to:

FOLLOWING THE TREND: as prices rise, anyone who follows the pattern will buy or sell short when they fall. This is based on the premise that ever-increasing and steadily declining prices will continue to do so.

CONTRARY INVESTMENT: This plan assumes that price rises are going to reverse and fall. During the increase, the opposite buys during the fall or short sells, with the express hope that the pattern will change.

SCALPING: This is a form where a speculator exploits the small price gaps created by the bid-ask spread. This technique involves typically rapidly, in minutes or even seconds, entering and exiting a position.

TRADING ON NEWS UPDATES: Traders who use this technique can purchase when good news is released and stay calm when bad news is reported. This may result in increased uncertainty, which may result in higher income and losses.

DAY TRADING IS HARD TO MASTER

Time, ability, and discipline are required. Many of those who attempt it fail, but the strategies mentioned above and guidance will help you create a successful plan. You will significantly improve your possibilities of beating the odds with enough preparation and regular performance evaluation.

Biggest Mistakes to Avoid While Day Trading

The high influence round of retail trading just got all the more energizing. With day trading sessions on, brokers are making brisk additions (and misfortunes) all in a limited capacity to focus time. A little information is a dangerous thing.

With satisfactory skill, discipline and a methodology that depends on choices, you also can win the prize (and score the objective) in the business sectors.

Averaging Down: The Flip-Side

Averaging down is certifiably not a decent method to climb in day trading sessions. While most brokers attempt to keep this from occurring, it unavoidably does. There are numerous issues with averaging down.

The first is that a losing position is held, which demonstrates expensive as far as time, yet also exertion and cash. A superior place is a stage up the cash stepping stool, and day trading is tied in with envisioning the successes (and the misfortunes) before they occur. For each dollar or rupee lost, more significant profits are required for capital to bringing back disasters.

For example, for a half misfortune supported, a 100% addition must be made to even things out. Averaging down in such a circumstance can prompt massive accidents or edge calls. This is because patterns can wait in any event, when merchants are fluid all the more so if capital is being included as the position moves out of winning additions.

Informal investors are likewise touchy to issues, and the brief timeframe outline for exchanges converts into circumstances that can be chased as they happen.

It's imperative to leave awful trades as fast as it is to enter significant transactions. Informal investors ought to be alert about how news occasions are moving the market and what course is the pattern taking it in.

Taking a situation before a news declaration can hurt a broker's possibility of accomplishment. There is no income sans work... it's tied in with trying sincerely and thinking brilliant.

Don't Fully Rely on News.

A news feature may hit the business sectors, which, at that point, begin to move quickly. This doesn't mean you will win cash. If you don't have a healthy preparing plan, trading resembles betting. News declarations lead to freezing responses and enthusiastic reactions, something which genuinely hurts day trading.

Trust that Volatility will Lessen

Informal investors should ensure that instability dies down, and there is a particular pattern for creating after news declarations have been made. Fewer liquidity concerns, the more successful administration of assets is conceivable. Stable value bearing is accordingly likely.

Try not to Risk More Than You Can Afford to Lose

Over the top chance doesn't hold any profits, and the hazard remunerates proportion must be agreeable generally dealers will lose over the long haul, something not for the most part connected with day trading. Regardless of the timeframe, merchants should chance close to 1% of capital inside a solitary exchange. Proficient dealers additionally try under 1% of the money. Day trading likewise implies additional thoughtfulness regarding a day by day hazard most extreme that should be executed. Day by day, chance most extreme can associate with 1 percent or less of the capital and proportional to average day by day benefit overtime of state, one month. By utilizing the hazard greatest, dealers guarantee that they don't stake beyond what they can stand to lose. Forex influence can immediately turn into a double edged sword, and ridiculous desires originate from shifted sources.

Acknowledge that the Market Can Be Illogical

Trading desires are regularly forced available. We think as far as what we want as opposed to the right trading course. The market isn't keen on what an individual needs. To put it, long just as medium-term cycles, markets can be unpredictable, relying on trading conditions. To alter for changes in the market, you have to define a trading plan and see whether it yields relentless outcomes. Acknowledge what the market carries on like. Keep in mind that capital development after some time can be joined by an increment in position size to yield higher dollar returns. New techniques can be executed with the least funding in any case. New systems would then be able to produce positive outcomes. As time extends and day trading advances, you may need to alter your procedure.

Entering Day Trading without a Plan Can be Disastrous

A typical mix-up made by merchants is entering the exchange without a compelling arrangement. Trading without a method prompts botches, particularly if you don't have the foggiest idea what you are getting into. Security against misfortunes implies modifying passage exit and in particular, departure cost or stop a disaster.

Try not to Leave Out the Margins

Day trading can represent the moment of truth, relying on the margin. At the point when you obtain from an intermediary to buy protections, a margin is that significant section of the exchange which can build benefits. A margin can be an essential partner for informal investors whenever utilized successfully. Trade with the cash you have, not money you acquired.

Try not to Chase Trades

A typical mistake during day trading is to pursue exchanges. As opposed to focusing on relentless and stable returns, informal investors might be enticed to pursue quick moving stocks. Getting more from the business than they can manage, this will clear out the unofficial investors' record and give day trading terrible notoriety. Pursuing exchanges when day trading stocks shoot up can prompt falling fortunes. If you pass up a share, don't continue it in the expectations that you can make up for the lost time.

Not getting Markets or Limiting Orders can Have Consequences

There is continuously a hurl up among the market and farthest point requests. While showcase request is a request to buy or sell the stock at current market rates, limit request licenses foundation of most extreme or negligible cost for trading security. Market requests can be filled quickly. However, the market ought not to control the demand. So also, limit requests can allow the parameters to be controlled. Regardless of whether farthest point requests or market orders sound useful to you, you should be sure that you can't miss a quick-moving stock to spare a couple of bucks — high stocks which are fluid grant the utilization of either market or point of confinement request.

Cling to Tips, Pay the Price

In what may appear to be irrational, it is crucial to recall that the individuals who need to assist you with requiring not to be your closest companions. Market witnesses frequently have plans, and nothing approaches reasonable trading. Active informal investors consider what they need to gather and make decisions in like manner. They don't get influenced by what others think.

Declining to Cut Losses Can Be Expensive

The human instinct is innately confident. This implies informal investors could be seeking a turnaround. This can be a deadly mix-up. Refusal to cut misfortunes can hurt your record. If your stock has traveled south, there is no compelling reason to proceed with it on a voyage to no place. Keep small misfortunes from transforming into bigger ones.

Timing is Everything in Day Trading

Trading too soon or late, excessively little or a lot of can be heartbreaking. Keep in mind that an initial couple of moments of trading are always confounded. The challenge towards the opening or closing bell is consistent with institutional speculators and high recurrence trading specialists at the end of the day, the massive fish in the ocean.

So, if you swim in too far, don't hope to remain above water since day trading isn't just about making benefits, it is additionally about staying away from misfortunes. At the point when markers become rough, ensure you step back.

Order is Everything

In the business sectors, discipline is needed to be a superior informal investor. Create exacting principles and don't depend on feelings.

Casual investors can likewise utilize specialized investigation. For instance, stochastics can be used to graph if a stock is finished or under exchange.

New Traders Look for Magic, Experts Know Better

Try not to search for an enchantment projectile or a wonder fix in day trading, because there is none. Tuning in to the outlines is as significant as tuning in to the news, and there is no simple method to play markets. Technique and control are expected to ensure you gain benefits.

Clueless Day Traders Lack Knowledge

An informal investor ought not to believe that anybody can profit in the business sectors. To be fruitful, you need preparation. A reliably winning merchant begins with paper trading and studies it hard enough to find how the market functions. Experiencing preparing for day trading can be as escalated and far-reaching as a doctoral qualification course!

Day Trading is All About Taming the Lion

Making cash off little variations in the cost of stock requires ability and inside and out comprehension. Rapid web associations and a lot of nerve can guarantee day trading turns out to be anything but difficult to complete. Be that as it may, having a stable and sure approach is additionally significant. Much like a creature can detect dread, so can a market. You should resemble a lion tamer... certain and intense.

Think of a Business Plan

Day trading systems are a business recommendation like salary generation. Marketable strategies ought to incorporate a rundown of hardware should have been fruitful, the arrangement of day trading instructional classes and projection of insignificant gainfulness over the short and long haul. Monitoring the financial backing would not be a poorly conceived notion either. This incorporates a record of costs connected with day trading.

Have a Solid Trading Philosophy

You have to recognize execution measurements and find which techniques work best for you while day trading. This incorporates characterizing what gives you an edge over others, distinguishing the exchange of exchange you are hoping to start and characterizing the leave methodology. It is likewise imperative to have the option to evaluate when you should close your position.

Consider Losses

In a one-day coordinate, it is absurd to expect to have immaculate batting standards. Day trading includes tolerating the misfortunes as much as valuing the successes. Working on trading is significant and gratitude to current advancements and day trading strategies, it is likewise simple. Markets include a think or swim approach since sinking is simpler than enduring, particularly for first time informal investors.

Pursue a Trading Strategy

It is not difficult to take care of business and become involved with feelings. This can prompt perilous day trading exercises like drive selling or purchasing. You have to create a trading system that guarantees achievement, not disappointment. Above all, you have to keep your feelings out.

Try not to Change Your Strategy Too Often

Commonly, informal investors will attempt to change a methodology since it doesn't appear to work. They don't consider external components, for example, advertising elements of unpredictability. This is their hindrance.

Utilize the News as well

Look at money-related news reports so you can make out what is occurring in the business sectors regularly. Investigate each exchange the setting of news you get and pick fruitful and beneficial exchanges.

Keep up a Trading Diary

A trading diary can assist you with monitoring misfortunes and gains in a composed way. You can even keep an electronic journal if you think that it's easier.

Continuously Do Post-Trade Analysis

You have to adjust to the changing markets, and this is just conceivable if you alter your techniques accordingly. The changing elements and inherent instability of the demand must be comprehended, not dreaded. If desires were steeds, informal investors would ride! Sadly, the inverse is also valid. In this way, utilize a stop misfortune with each request to stay away from a terrible exchange. Use limit arranges well and doesn't pursue the pattern, search for stable returns. Not recognizing what point to profit by the business sectors is maybe the most concerning issue in day trading. Utilizing standards of brain science or social fund is significant. You have to recognize what works and (all the more critically) what doesn't. There is a contrast between self-conviction and predictions that denotes the difference between day trading and betting!

CHAPTER 3:

MORE TIPS FOR BEGINNERS ON DAY TRADING

When starting a career, when you're a day trading novice, there's a lot to learn. Here are a few more tips/strategies to help you as you start your journey in the right direction. Such suggestions will give you the right equipment and software to set up, help you select what to trade as well as when to trade, show you how much money you need, how to manage risk, and how to implement a trading strategy maximally.

CHOOSING A DAY TRADING MARKET

You may even have a business in mind that you want to trade as a novice day trader. The job of a day trader is to find a pattern repeating (or repeating enough to make a profit) and afterward utilize it.

Company shares, like Walmart (WMT) as well as Apple (AAPL), are stocks. Investors are trading currencies like the euro and the US dollar (EUR / USD) on the forex market. Trade offers a wide range of futures, and futures are often focused on commodities or indexes. You can exchange 500 movements of crude oil, gold, or S&P on the futures market.

There's no better one sector than another. It boils down to what and what you can barely manage to trade. The forex market needs day-to-day trading with the least money. You could start with just as few hundred dollars, although it is suggested, to begin with at least $500.

Trading other futures markets, such as the S&P 500 E-mini (ES), a very common contract for day trading futures, requires only $1,000 to get started. Nonetheless, it is suggested to begin with at least $2,500.

Stocks require daily trading of about $25,000, making them an option that is more capital-intensive.

Although there is a need for more money to exchange shares today, this does not make it a better market or worse market than the rest.

But if you don't have to trade $25,000 (and can't keep your account above $25,000), then stocks are probably not the best day trading market for you. If you have more than $25,000, shares will be a viable market for day trading.

All markets offer great potential for profit. Therefore, it often comes down to how much capital you need to get started. Choose a market, so you can begin to focus your research on that market and not waste your energy learning things about any other markets that might not be useful in your chosen market.

Don't try to master all markets simultaneously. This will split your focus, and it may take longer to make money. It's easier to adapt and know other markets when you learn how to make money in one market. Therefore, be cautious. Not all markets need to be understood at once. If you want, you can later learn about other markets.

Tools for Day Trading Beginners

A LAPTOP OR DESKTOP. It is better to have two screens, but not required. The machine should have enough memory and a fast enough processor to prevent lagging or crashing while running your trading software (discussed later). You don't need a top-of-the-line machine, but neither do you want to make it cheap. Technology and devices are continually changing, so be sure to keep your computer up to date. On a trading day, a slow machine's hazard can be expensive, particularly if it crashes while you're in business, causing you to miss trading, or its slowness causes you to get stuck in business.

A SECURE AND RELATIVELY FAST INTERNET CONNECTIVITY. Day traders should use at least one cable or ADSL style internet connection. Such types of services vary in price, so look for at least a mid-range internet package.

Your internet provider's slowest speed may do the job, but if you have multiple web pages and applications running (using the internet), you can find that your trading platform is not updating as quickly as it is supposed to, and that can cause problems. Start with an internet package of mid-range and check it out. If required, you can change your internet speed later. If your internet speed is going down a lot, it's a problem.

A GOOD TRADING WEBSITE. A trading site perfect for your day-trading market and fashion. When you're just starting, your goal is not to find the ideal platform. Install and try a range of trading platforms. You're not going to have a well-developed trading style yet since you're a novice. So, your trading platform may change periodically over your career, or you may adjust how it is set up to accommodate your success in trading. NinaTrader is a standard day trading platform for traders of futures and forex. There are plenty of websites for stock trading. Finally, try some of the stuff your broker has to sell and see which one you like best.

A BROKER. There's a dealer. Your broker sets up your business and pays a commission or fee on your company in return. Day traders want to concentrate on low-fee brokers as high commission costs could destroy a day's trading strategy's profitability. That said, it is not always possible to have the lowest fee broker. If you have a question, you want a broker to be there to provide help. If the company can help you save hundreds or thousands of dollars when you have a software breakdown and can't get out of your business, a few cents extra on a commission is worth it. Major Banks are usually not the best option for day traders, although some offer trading accounts. Fees tend to be typically higher at significant banks, and smaller brokers often offer today traders more flexible prices and commission structures.

Best Times for Day Trading

As a day trader, both as a novice and as a specialist, your life is based on reliability. Trading during the same hours each day is one way to generate continuity.

While some day traders trade for an entire regular session (for example, for the US stock market within 9:30 a.m. to 4 p.m. EST), many trade for a portion of the day. Trading is quite popular among day traders just two to three hours a day. Here are the hours that you want to focus on.

The best time for day trading of stocks is the first one to two hours after opening, and the last hour before closing. From 9:30 a.m. to around 11:30 a.m. EST is a two-hour trading window that you want to use to get better.

This is the most unpredictable time of the day, providing the most significant swings in value and the most significant opportunity for gain: the day's last hour, 3 p.m. to around 4 p.m. Typically, EST is also a good time for trading, as there are also some significant moves. Deal in the morning session if you only want to deal for an hour or two.

For day trading futures, close the opening is a good time to day trade. Active prospects see some trading activity around the clock, so good day trading opportunities usually start a bit earlier compared to stock market.

If day trading futures specifies on trading between 8:30 a.m. and 11 a.m. EST, future markets do have official closes at different times, but the last hour of trading in a futures contract also typically offers sizable moves for day traders to capitalize on.

Throughout the week, the forex market operates 24 hours a day. The EUR/USD is by far the most famous pair of day traders. Usually, between 0600 and 1700 GMT, it sees the most volatility. Day traders are supposed to trade inside these hours. Often, between

1200 and 1500 GMT considers the most significant price swings, so this is a successful time for day traders. London and the US markets are open during this period, exchanging the euro and the US dollar.

You don't have to work all day as a day trader. When dealing just two or three hours a day, you'll probably find more flexibility.

More Tips on Managing Your Day Trading Risk

You've chosen a market, set up computers and tools, and often you know what's right for day trading. You need to learn how to manage the risk before you even start thinking about selling. There are two ways for day traders to manage risk: trade risk and daily risk.

Trade risk is how much of a trade you are willing to risk. Ideally, any transaction that risks 1 percent or less of your money is okay. This is done by choosing an entry point and then setting a stop loss that will get you out of business if you start going too much against yourself.

The hazard is also influenced by the degree to which you take a position, so learn how to measure the appropriate stock, forex, or futures place size. No single trade will expose you to more than 1 percent capital loss by factoring your position size, your entry price, as well as your stop-loss rate.

Check the regular threat, as well. Just as you don't want your account to be impaired by a single trade (hence the 1 percent rule), you don't want to destroy your week or month one day. Therefore, set a limit on the regular loss.

One choice is to set it at 3 percent of your money. When you threaten 1 percent or less for each trade, you'd have to lose three or more trades (with no winners) to suffer 3 percent loss. This shouldn't happen very often with a sound strategy. Stop trading for the day after you hit your daily cap.

Set your regular loss cap equal to your average winning day once you're consistently profitable. When you typically make $500 on winning days, for example, on losing days, you are allowed to lose $500. Stop trading if you lose more than that. The reasoning is that we want to keep small regular losses so that a typical winning day can quickly recover the loss.

Practicing Strategies for Day Trading Beginners

- Don't try to learn all about trading at once when you start. You don't have to know everything. As a day trader, you need only one technique which you regularly execute. You don't need a school or academic degree, and you don't need to read hundreds of books to do that.
- Find a technique that will provide an entry process, set a stop loss, and take profits. Then

go to a demo account to focus on implementing the plan.

- This means that if you want, even when the market is open, you can practice all day.
- Regardless of which sector you are trading, open a demo account and start the plan. Learning a technique is not the same as being able to put it into practice. There are no two days in the markets that are the same, so it takes effort to be able to see the business setups and conduct the company without hesitation. Practice with minimal capital for at least three months before scaling in your trading. Only if you are in a line of lucrative demo results for at least three months will you turn to live trade.
- Remain focused on that particular strategy, and that only trading your selected market during the time you've chosen to trade.

MOVING FROM DEMO TO LIVE TRADING

Some traders note a quality decrease when switching from demo trading to live trading. Demo trading is undoubtedly a good practice ground for evaluating whether a strategy is feasible, but it cannot accurately mimic the actual market, nor does it generate the emotional trauma that many traders experience when placing real money at risk.

Therefore, when you find that when you start living (compared to the demo), your trading doesn't go very well, you know this is normal.

As you get more familiar with real money trading, raise your position size to the 1 percent level or slightly above. Take your focus back to what you already did consistently and correctly apply your techniques. Concentrating on consistency and execution may help dilute some of the intense emotions that may harm your business.

The word for Day Trading Beginners

Choose a market that you want and can manage to trade, and after that, set up the proper equipment and software for yourself. Choose a day that you can trade daily and only trade during that time; usually, the best trading times every day are between big openings and closings of the market.

Manage your threat, every day and on every trade. So, again and again, execute this plan. You don't need to learn all about productivity in exchange. There is just one technique you need to be able to develop that makes money.

Until trying to learn others, focus on winning with one technique. In a demo account, sharpen your skills, but remember it's not exactly like a real business. A bumpy ride is usual for several months if you turn to actual capital trading. To stabilize the emotions, emphasis on accuracy, and execution.

CHAPTER 4:

DAY TRADING STRATEGIES A TO Z

This Chapter will give definitions of day trading and intraday trading, and it will explore different day trading systems, the way traders make profits with day trading systems, some ideas for the best Forex day trading systems, and some great tips for you to use in your daily trading.

Intra-day trading is a series of Forex day trading strategies allowing professional traders to enter and exit the same day trading. Given that stocks can only move so far within one day, traders of intra-day use comparatively more aggressive trading strategies to maximize their desired profits.

Day trading Forex tactics are filled with more activity and allow traders throughout the day to be present at the trading station. It is commonly accepted that a trader operates within the shorter time frame, the higher the risk they are susceptible to. This is why day trading can be identified as being one of the currency markets' most risky approaches. What raises the risk is not the various Forex trading strategies that day traders need to use. Yes, for almost every interval out there, the underlying rationale is the same. Instead, Forex day trade rules tend to be stricter and more unforgiving for those who don't obey them.

Errors are more costly and are likely to occur more often, as the transaction itself would be of a higher frequency.

PROCEDURES & STRATEGIES

The two considerations that no intra-day trader can do without are volatility and liquidity, irrelevant of any of the Forex day trading plan that they intend to use.

It may seem like something good for any trader, but they are much more reliant on short-term traders. The frequency of market movements is uncertainty. High volatility is a must when investing in the short term.

It limits the choice of pieces, depending on the courses, to the major currency pairs, and a few cross pairs. Talking of sessions, understanding when to trade is as important as knowing what to sell because volatility is dependent on course. Liquidity is very much germane. Trading intra-day is very accurate. A long-term trader can choose here to throw ten pips and slice ten pips. Since ten pips could be the entire gain expected for a deal, a short-term trader can't.

SCALPING STRATEGY

Scalping is a day-trading Forex technique aimed at achieving several small profits based on the potential minimal price shifts. Scalpers go for transactions in amounts, opening up almost 'on a hunch' as there is no other way to access through the chaos of the market. Scalping can be thrilling and highly risky at the same time. Scalpers need to achieve a high trading likelihood of balancing the low reward risk ratio. Probably the most challenging part of scalping is the immediate termination of losing trades. A scalper cannot afford to hope for the return of the market.

If you want to become a scalper, consider developing a sixth sense of the business–look for dynamic devices, better liquidity, and a high rate of execution. When perfected, scalping in any financial market is probably the most profitable strategy. Only the adjacent uncertainties stop from becoming the best strategy for Forex day trading.

REVERSE TRADING STRATEGY

Often known as pullback trading, counter-trend trading, or fading is reverse trading.

The risk comes from the fundamental principle of counter-trend trading. To predict their power, a reverse trader must be able to identify possible pullbacks with a high probability. It does require a lot of business experience and understanding, although it is not impossible. A particular case of the reverse trading strategy can be called the 'Daily Pivots' approach, as it specializes in trading the daily low and daily high pullbacks and reversals.

MOMENTUM TRADING STRATEGY

This is a pretty simple day-trading Forex strategy that specializes in looking for large price movements coupled with high volumes and going forward trading. In momentum trading, a high degree of trading discipline is required to be able to wait for just the best opportunity to enter a position and to maintain active control to remain focused and spot the exiting signal.

Day trading is often declared as the best way to make a return on your Forex trading portfolio. What the advertisements fail to mention, however, is that it's the most robust technique to learn. As a result, most beginners are trying to fail.

Forex Day Trading Systems

Forex day trading is done exclusively within one day, and trading will always be closed before the trade ends that same day. Those who trade this way are called day traders. Generally, a Forex day trading system consists of a series of logical signals that influence the trader's purchasing or selling decisions on each of their daily sessions. The system can help traders manage the market in a much more productive and comfortable manner to allow them to gain more money.

In the past, Forex day trading operations were limited to financial institutions and qualified speculators. Most day traders are banks and investment firms' staff, who specialized in private capital and fund management. Nevertheless, the day trading system has now gained popularity among 'at-home traders' with the advent of electronic trading and margin trading systems.

Today almost anyone can trade Forex from the comfort of their own homes with easy access to Forex trading. For different reasons, people choose to go into day trading. Nonetheless, the fact that day traders do not pay the 'Swap' (a cost that is paid when a position is kept open overnight) is a variable that is likely to have made this practice much more common in recent years.

HOW FOREX DAY TRADERS MAKE PROFIT

Day traders manipulate large amounts of capital to gain by taking advantage of small price fluctuations between highly liquid indices, shares, or currencies. Such investors, in other words, are not searching for large price drops and peaks. Instead, they are content with low, moderate movements, but their scales of exchange are higher than those held by traders who invest for more extended periods. As a day trader, the main goal is to generate a significant amount of pips within a given day. Ideally, both of the highs and lows of the capital will produce returns. The entries in the different Forex day trading systems utilize similar types of methods used in normal trading-the only distinction is timing and approach. You usually expect to make less money per trade with day trading, but you expect far more trades to be done.

METATRADER SUPREME EDITION

Having the right forum and a reliable broker are tremendously important trading aspects. Admiral Markets is an award-winning broker offering the ability to trade on the Forex market, trading with CFDs, investing in stocks and ETFs, and more. With only the state-of-the-art trading platform MetaTrader, all this is facilitated. Admiral Markets provides an enhanced version of the application known as the MetaTrader Supreme Edition for MetaTrader 4 and MetaTrader 5.

With MTSE, professional traders will improve their trading capabilities by leveraging the latest real-time market data, feedback from experienced trading experts, and a variety of additional features such as the convenient 'Mini Trader' function – allowing traders to buy or sell inside a small window without needing to visit the trading platform whenever they want to make a change.

BEST FOREX DAY TRADING SYSTEMS

There is a wide range of Forex day exchanging frameworks - it is significant not to mistake them for exchanging procedures. The fundamental distinction between a structure and a process is that a framework, for the most part, characterizes a style of an exchanging, while a technique is progressively graphic and gives nitty-gritty data increasingly - to be specific section and leave focuses, pointers and time allotments. A concise review of probably the most ordinarily utilized frameworks is given underneath (Please note: scalping, blurring, and force are exchanging procedures also):

Scalping: In this framework, the purchasing or selling happens immediately after the exchange accomplishes benefit. In this exchanging type, the objective is to achieve profit when you are up by only a couple of pips. You can hope to exchange a great deal and produce a severe colossal volume. Be that as it may, the pay per exchange is relatively little.

Fading: This framework includes the shorting of stocks, a record, or a cash pair, following upward moves. In this type of day exchanging, the value target is set when purchasers begin to step in once more. You mean to make pips available movements that attempt to reestablish the past cost of an advantage.

Day by day Pivots: In this framework, the benefit is increased through the unpredictability of the day by day costs of advantages. The purchasing or selling happens during the low time of the day, and the shutting of the exchange occurs at the high time of the day. The value focus has a comparable example, as referenced previously.

Momentum: In this sort of Forex day exchanging framework, exchanging is typically performed on news discharges, or by finding the solid moves which are inclining, and which are upheld by high volumes. The value focus in this procedure is the point at which the amount begins to decrease, and the presence of bearish candles happens. You are commonly investigating gaining an advantage a couple of hours before the news is discharged, and afterward, along these lines disposing of it after the market has moved enough into your bearing.

CONTINUATION ON BEST FOREX DAY TRADING SYSTEMS

As you may have realized at this point, managing a day exchanging framework can be a severe test. There is a long way to go and get ready, for vast numbers of us don't have the opportunity, experience, or information to do. Accordingly, when you are beginning, it's valuable to recognize what the best-exchanging framework will be. While it's always decent to have a Forex trading procedure to work from, you have to have something past that, to help you measure up and start winning some capital.

Since the best Forex exchanging framework for you will accommodate your market and needs, finding the perfect one can be difficult work. However, the best activity is to recollect that most Forex exchanging frameworks are worked around different systems and will, in general, run with their very own establishments, acute angles, and attributes.

The group of dealers utilizing day exchanging frameworks is stacked with such a significant number of various individuals, with differing arrangements. Accordingly, finding the most fabulous day trading framework is hard – and it relies upon such a substantial amount of little factors that there is no complete response to give to you. In any case, you can have a sense of security in the information that finding the correct exchanging framework will commonly originate from directing your exploration.

Having the option to manage what the best FX day exchanging framework is for you additionally originates from your very own understanding – what do you at present think about the real system? Do you need something that can assist you with getting into the framework from the very start? Or, do you require something that will give your current information a push the right way?

Whatever you pick, you have to begin looking at the FX exchanging frameworks that are out there – some of them will make crazy guarantees that you can't trust, yet it should be simple enough to begin settling on the correct decisions and choices dependent on how practical they sound. Keep in mind, and the program needs to look bona fide – if it's not worked around essential data and doesn't give you the subtleties that you can profit by in the long haul, move onto the next one.

Be sure to glance around and locate the correct parity for your individual needs – what you know, what you can manage, and what you are happy to contribute will all direct what the top exchanging frameworks are for you. As it were, the best structure for trading Forex is the most reasonable one.

With regards to exchanging the present moment, you would need it to be advantageous, and you would need to feel sure utilizing it, as this is an action you would perform for a couple of hours consistently. It is recommended that you evaluate the entirety of the previously mentioned frameworks on a demo exchanging account first, before taking part in live record exchanging. This is appropriate in any event, for experienced dealers that are thinking about changing starting with one framework then onto the next.

MORE ON FOREX DAY TRADING TIPS

The act of day exchanging is the least famous among proficient brokers and the most mainstream among beginner merchants. If you are a beginner, here is the most distinguished Forex day trading tip of all: get some involvement in long haul exchanging. First attempt to substantiate yourself by being reliably beneficial with a live record for a moderately significant period, utilizing long haul exchanging procedures.

The more experienced you become, the lower the time spans you will have the option to exchange on effectively. Assuming in any case, despite everything you choose to or even unknowingly slip into day exchanging, here are a couple of Forex day trading tips that may enable you to out. Day trading for novices, as a rule, begins with investigating. They will, in general, pay special mind to various approaches to improve their exchanging and commit an immense measure of time to scan for the correct beginning stage.

FX learner dealers are continually looking for the ideal pointer or exchanging framework that furnishes arrangements with a 100 percent achievement rate. Indeed, even some accomplished proficient brokers do it occasionally. Sadly, impeccable structures don't exist, and the main genuine 'Sacred goal' is appropriate cash the executives.

The most critical day exchanging programming for learners is the MetaTrader exchanging stage, as it offers to exchange with miniaturized scale parcels. Here are a couple of tips if you are trading with Admiral Markets:

1. Open a demo account utilizing the MT4 day exchanging stage.

2. Pick one of the methodologies that appeared in the segment of the online course of the Admiral Markets site.

3. Exchange the picked framework on a demo account until you are reliably productive.

4. Attempt to exchange the demo account precisely as you would trade with a live record.

5. The propensities you create in the demo ought to intuitively continue into your live exchanging.

Build up a severe exchanging design and tail it carefully to deal with your dangers appropriately. Brilliant merchants practice hazard the executives' procedures inside their exchange, to limit and deal with the risks successfully. As referenced above, day trading Forex is more dangerous than lengthy haul exchanging, for the most part, in light of the faster pace and higher recurrence of exchanges. Informal investors will participate in general, experience more weight, and must have the option to settle on choices rapidly and acknowledge full duty regarding the outcomes.

A Forex exchanging plan is a flat out must for an informal investor. Look out for averaging down. Averaging down alludes to keeping a losing exchange open
for a long time. To stay away from it, cut losing exchanges agreement with pre-arranged leave systems. Keep in mind, averaging down when day

exchanging Forex eats up your benefits, yet in addition, your exchanging time.

Shouldn't something be said about a stop-misfortune? There are two sorts every informal investor must think about utilizing.

A physical stop-misfortune request is set at a value level as per the hazard resistance, which you should know from your exchanging plan. Around 1-2 percent is a decent level for this. Essentially, this is the most you can bear to lose in one exchange. The other kind is a psychological stop-misfortune – and this one is implemented by the merchant when they get the inclination that something is turning out badly.

Have you at any point entered an exchange and watched the market make a surprising turn, and afterward, all of a sudden understood that the exchange is nothing worth mentioning and it's time to cash out? That is a psychological stop. The stunt isn't mistaking it for alarm. That is the reason both physical and mental stops should be thoroughly considered before entering an exchange, and not afterward.

Retail informal investors, especially the individuals who deal with their own instead of another person's cash, have another standard that their stop-misfortunes must consent to. They set the most extreme misfortune for each day that they can bear to withstand monetarily and rationally. If that point is ever reached, they continue to expel themselves from the market for the day by and large. They realize that horrible originates from passionate exchanging. Unpracticed brokers, interestingly, don't have the foggiest idea when to get out.

They regularly feel constrained to make up misfortunes before the day is finished, which prompts 'vengeance exchanging,' which never closes well for them. Exemptions to every one of these principles are conceivable, yet should be dealt with explicit consideration, and the outcomes must be acknowledged with full duty. Great results must not serve to strengthen standard exceptional cases. Terrible consequences ought to be considered as a decent update regarding why these guidelines exist.

The pattern may have the option to support itself longer than you can stay fluid. How about we consider unpredictability spikes blended in with drops in liquidity. At the point when news discharges are expected, brokers should avoid exchanging by and large, except if these are the particular economic situations that their exchanging technique requires.

Try not to exchange around the significant news reports as the outcomes could be appalling. The reality is this – regardless of whether you figure out how to recognize what the news will be, there is no real way to anticipate how the market will respond in the first couple of hours. Bullish news can cause a bearish market snap and the other way around.

In the long run, the market will come back to its pattern, yet until it does, nature isn't protected enough to exchange. Deciding your ideal day exchanging framework for monetary forms is a hard errand. It takes a ton of experimentation, yet it can pay back colossally as well. When you have decided on an ideal framework, it is then time to choose the most fitting procedure for it.

A technique will furnish you with progressively nitty-gritty data for executing your day exchanges while depending on the characterized specialized pointers and articles. What is likewise prescribed is to take a stab at actualizing a couple of frameworks, and look at which one is the most fascinating and agreeable for you. Try not to flee; the primary thought while choosing a framework is to be sure about what you are doing.

Additionally, remember that a dealer probably won't have the option to secure their record with stop arranges around the news. If there is no liquidity available, and the request won't close. It will keep dozing until the most readily accessible counter-party is happy to exchange. So essentially, it is just at their value that you will trade. Be that as it may, the most crucial day trading methodology Forex is consistently to trade at your cost.

I hope you did enjoy reading this chapter and got a better comprehension of Forex day trading systems and strategies.

CHAPTER 5:

DAY TRADING SIGNALS

Day trading signals are, basically, exchange ideas showing the market drifts progressively. Exchanging messages are utilized by fledgling and expert merchants the same. Most forex signals incorporate the position type (purchase or sell) just as the assume benefit and stop misfortune levels. FX Leaders gives a flag on forex sets, products, records, and digital currencies.

Pursue the live flag and physically duplicate them to your exchanging stage by opening a purchase/sell position as indicated by the information of the dynamic sign.

FX Leaders forex signals are exchange thoughts. The merchant gets the position (purchase/sell) posted on the forex signals page together with the stop misfortune (SL) and takes benefit (TP) levels. Traders should duplicate the exchange at the market cost when the sign goes live.

Notwithstanding 'Dynamic' (live) signals, FX Leaders utilizes 'Prepare' messages. This sort of sign is distributed to tell dealers when the FX Leaders expert group sees a great specialized diagram arrangement or a significant occasion, and are going to open a vital sign.

As a superior part, you will get email messages and notices on your cell phone, so you never miss an exchange. Moreover, you will right away get the full sign subtleties which incorporates the time the sign was given, passage value, the instrument to exchange (forex pair/ware/record/cryptographic money), sort of sign (purchase/sell), and the assume benefit and stop misfortune levels.

There is a wide range of forex signal administrations accessible. Numerous individual forex dealers give flag through the MT4/MT5 stages or their intermediaries as exchange copiers, for example, ZuluTrade or eToro. At FX Leaders, we have a group of expert merchants and examiners who create a new forex flag each day. We are pleased with our administrations and execution and are always attempting to improve them.

In 2017/2018, FX Leaders presented new exchanging sign-on products, records, and cryptographic forms of money, enabling merchants to expand their exchanging portfolios. If you have been following FX Leaders, you may have

seen the association between our live market refreshes and our forex signals. Other than giving signals, we attempt to go with the sign with the methodologies and explanations for them.

You don't need to pursue every one of our signals by the book. Forex signals are exchange thoughts, so it's ideal to think about them like this and at whatever point conceivable to expand your benefits. Stop misfortune and take benefit levels are given to outline the range wherein the market is relied upon to move dependent on a particular pattern. If your exchanging technique focuses on additional gains, don't restrain your potential. Expand your take benefit (TP) target or evacuate everything together to amplify benefits.

Our signal is overseen physically since they are made by our accomplished examiners who apply diverse manual exchanging methodologies to the business sectors. This is against other sign suppliers whose signs are created naturally. There are upsides and downsides for the two administrations, which we clarify in our "Forex Signals – Auto versus Manual" article. We lean toward manual flag as we see more an incentive in human knowledge than in human-made reasoning.

FX Leaders' master experts utilize both short and long haul exchanging investigation and systems. Because of this, various kinds of merchants can use FX Leaders' exchanging signals as the sign can coordinate diverse exchanging styles, for example, specialized examination exchanging, crucial investigation exchanging, day exchanging, and swing trading.

CHAPTER 6

DAY TRADING FOREX

Many individuals like exchanging remote monetary forms on the foreign trade (forex) showcase since it requires minimal funding to begin day exchanging. Forex exchanges 24 hours per day during the week and offers a great deal of benefit potential because of the influence gave by forex agents. Forex trading can be very unstable, and an unpracticed dealer can lose a lot of money. The following situation shows the potential, utilizing a hazard controlled forex day exchanging procedure.

FOREX DAY TRADING RISK MANAGEMENT

Each active forex informal investor deals with their hazard; it is one of, if not the, most pivotal components of continuous gainfulness.

To begin, you should keep your hazard on each exchange little, and 1 percent or less is regular. This means if you have a $3,000 account, you shouldn't lose more than $30 on a solitary exchange. That may appear to be little. However, misfortunes do happen, and even a decent day-exchanging methodology will see a series of setbacks. Hazard is overseen utilizing a stop-misfortune request, which will be examined in the scenario segments below.

FOREX DAY TRADING STRATEGY

While a procedure can have numerous segments and can be broke down for success in different manners, a technique is regularly positioned dependent on its success rate and hazard/remunerate proportion.

WIN RATE

Your success rate speaks to the number of exchanges you win out a given absolute number of trades. Let's assume you win 55 out of 100 trades; your success rate is 55 percent. While it isn't required, having a success rate of over 50 percent is perfect for most informal investors, and 55 percent is adequate and feasible.

HAZARD/REWARD

Hazard/remunerate how much capital is being gambled to achieve a specific benefit. If a merchant loses ten pips on losing exchanges, but makes 15 on winning trades, she is building more on the victors than she's losing on failures. This implies that regardless of whether the broker just succeeds on half of her trades, she will be productive. Along these lines, making more on winning trades is likewise a key segment for which numerous forex informal investors endeavor.

A higher success rate for exchanges implies greater adaptability with your hazard/remunerate, and a high chance/compensate your success rate can be lower, you'd be happy.

THEORETICAL SCENARIO

A dealer has $5,000 in capital assets, and they have an average win pace of 55 percent on their exchanges. The hazard just 1 percent of their capital or $50 per trade. This is cultivated by utilizing a stop-misfortune request. For this situation, a stop-misfortune request is put five pips from the exchange section cost, and an objective is set eight pips away.

This implies the potential reward for each exchange is 1.6 occasions more noteworthy than the hazard (8/5). Keep in mind, and you need victors to be higher than washouts.

While exchanging a forex pair for two hours during a functioning time of day, it usually is conceivable to make around five round turn exchanges (round turn incorporates passage and leave) utilizing the above parameters. If there are 20 exchanging days a month, the broker is making 100 exchanges in a month.

EXCHANGING LEVERAGE

Forex representatives give influence up to 50:1 (more in individual nations). For this model, expect the broker is utilizing 30:1 control, as typically, that is all that anyone could need power for informal forex investors. Since the merchant has $5,000, and energy is 30:1, the broker can take positions worth up to $150,000. Hazard is as yet dependent on the first $5,000; this keeps the risk restricted to a little part of the stored capital.

Forex merchants regularly don't charge a commission, but instead, increment the spread between the offers and ask, hence making it increasingly hard to day exchange beneficially. ECN merchants offer a minimal range, making it more straightforward to exchange gainfully. However, they regularly charge about $2.50 for each $100,000 traded ($5 round turn).

EXCHANGING CURRENCY PAIRS

In case you are day trading a money pair like the GBP/USD, you can hazard $50 on each exchange, and each pip of development is worth $10 with a standard parcel (100,000 units worth of cash). Subsequently, you can take the place of one standard part with a 5-pip stop-misfortune request, which will keep the danger of misfortune to $50 on the exchange. That likewise implies a triumphant trade is worth $80 (8 pips x $10).

This gauge can show how a lot of an informal forex investor could make in a month by executing 100 exchanges:

55 exchanges were productive: 55 x $80 = $4,400

45 exchanges were failures: 45 x ($50) = ($2,250)

Net benefit is $4,400 - $2,250 = $2,150 if no commissions (win rate would almost certainly be lower however)

Net benefit is $2,150 - $500 = $1, 650 if utilizing a commission specialist (win rate would resemble be higher however)

Accepting a net benefit of $1,650, the arrival on the record for the month is 33 percent ($1,650/$5,000). This may appear to be exceptionally high, and it is a generally excellent return. See Refinements below to perceive how this arrival might be influenced.

SLIPPAGE LARGER THAN EXPECTED LOSS

It won't generally be conceivable to find five great day exchanges every day, particularly when the market is moving gradually for expanded periods.

Slippage is an inescapable piece of exchanging. It brings about a more significant misfortune than anticipated, in any event, when utilizing a stop-misfortune request. It's regular in quick-moving markets.

To represent slippage in the computation of your potential benefit, lessen the net profit by 10 percent (this is a high gauge for slippage, expecting you abstain from holding through significant financial information discharges). This would lessen the net benefit potential produced by your $5,000 exchanging money to $1,485 every month.

You can alter the situation above dependent on your usual stop misfortune and target, capital, slippage, win rate, position size, and commission parameters.

Do's And Don't's In Forex Trading

Many experienced and amateur merchants (more than you would think) don't get the abovementioned points. They are pursuing the cost in an endeavor not to miss a single pip of the move, in this way, not utilizing affirmations for their entrances. As such, they are virtually overlooking the guidelines of the procedure. Since this one resembles a decent arrangement, I will hop in somewhat before increasing more. This is when the cost doesn't do what you anticipate that it should do.

This is a subject that worries numerous brokers. See (below) the most significant Do's and Don't's Any Forex Trader Should Know.

Do's

Any forex merchant who is good to go to start trading in the business sectors ought to be prepared with a trading plan. The mainstays of effective forex lie with sound information and comprehension of the whole Foreign Exchange Trade Lifecycle.

To give a smooth beginning to their exchange business, one should remember the present money related market situation and concentrate the elements and lead fundamental research identified with forex exchange.

Another merchant ought to consistently start his exchange when the market shows a logically developing or down

Before starting a money exchange, he ought to consistently remember the increase and misfortune proportion.

Having sound information on the Fibonacci Analysis will assist a dealer with choosing the best time for his entrance or exit for beginning an exchange as it empowers them to predict the market variances.

A point by point specialized and critical investigation of the existing trading designs by utilizing graphs, continuation examples, or pattern inversion will be useful for another forex merchant.

The utilization of wise trading robots will assist them with achieving marvelous achievement.

Don't's

1. Never retribution the market after a losing exchange. Ever.

This isn't playing a computer game where you can vindicate when things don't go as you needed. There are no cheats. There is no restart. This is your cash we are discussing.

You go crazy and angry? Don't sweat it – the market will quiet you somewhere near gathering as much as you are happy to lose; if you feel disturbed, walk away. Take a walk, go to the rec center, do a couple of push-ups. Try not to stay dependent on feelings.

If you still don't get it, let me make the image more clear for you. You are in the ring battling Tyson. He tosses a couple of punches in your face (misfortune). Not all that solid; however, Mike realizes this is an inviting saving, so you are as yet aware (chance administration).

Presently, if you go distraught and start shouting at him, and if you attempt to vindicate for the punches from before WITHOUT following what your mentor told you, to be specific to keep your guard up and keep moving, what might occur? You will be taken out in the blink of an eye.

2. Try not to take incautious exchanges

You are watching the news. You hear something about rate increment, and you promptly open an exchange. Another model. You read your preferred blog.

This isn't the way it works. Try not to do it. Leave the rash choices for the gambling club. The choices that you make will influence your wallet and financial balance. Tolerance is presumably one of the hardest (if not the hardest) aptitudes each merchant must learn. It is undoubtedly among the primary three characteristics you should have. If there is nothing more than a wrong memory arrangement for seven days, don't exchange. It is smarter to be at equal the initial investment than in negative. Try not to constrain the market since you can't.

3. Try not to be eager

If you should, at any cost, pursue the movie till its last pip, feel free to do it. Call me in 3 weeks and tell me how you are getting along.

Try not to be that person, don't be that broker. Most importantly, apply the rule of making back the initial investment your exchanges once you are in a positive region. It is an incredible method to chance the free of your current transaction and allow it to run. Mentally it will assist you withholding your positions significantly more and as much as required as opposed to having the likelihood to lose on an exchange that was a champ.

The subsequent stage isn't to be voracious. If there is backing or opposition level 5 pips before your objective, put your goal there. Put it even a couple of pips before the S/R level. Ensure you do all that you can to transform your exchange into a champ. One hundred forty-two pips benefit is equivalent to 148 pips of gains, BUT it isn't equal to -70 pips misfortune.

4. Try not to have unreasonable desires

Trading is a business of insights, not assurances. You will have victories, and you will have failures. This is the truth. If you hope to have winning exchanges, trading isn't for you. Trading is tied in with finding the harmony among winning and losing such that we profit after 100 transactions.

Do not try to turn into a mogul in a half year if you have begun with a 5k account. Do not try and hope to have made 100k. Trading the business sectors resembles setting off to the rec center. It requires a great deal of tolerance and consistency. You can't deceive.

Regardless of whether you have the cash to do liposuction to get more fit, you won't be fat. That is fine, yet you won't be ripped off either. Do you see where I'm going with this? There is no other path around other than doing it the correct way – preparing, right nourishment, rest, regardless of how rich you are and what number of fitness coaches you procure. There is just one individual on the planet who can move your body – you.

If you need to make cash trading, the business sectors put the exertion, try sincerely, and one day, it will occur. Your future is in your grasp; don't pursue the ridiculous dreams that will leave you with empty pockets. There are sufficient dream dealers out there who are prepared to take your cash.

5. Try not to utilize tremendous influence

Influence, inessential words, implies acquired cash. Cash that isn't yours. This business has been planned and reshaped throughout the years ordinarily. A few changes were for good, some for awful. Having the option to utilize such immense use that intermediaries offer right now is a double edged sword. Influence in the hands of an accomplished dealer could be a weapon of mass annihilation. In any case, if you give a child a gun to play with, it won't be such a smart thought.

Try not to be the child with the weapon. Teach yourself. Know your rights, obligations, cutoff points, and edges. If you neglect to do so, your specialist will be incredibly content with you. They will even give you rewards on your next store.

6. Try not to exchange bits of gossip.

Don't take rash exchanges. Bits of gossip could be unsafe if they arrive at inappropriate ears. Try not to bounce into a trade because:

The rundown could continue forever; however, I trust you got my point. There is nothing incorrectly to update yourself as often as possible on news and new patterns. Adhere to your arrangement and procedure; there's nothing more to it. If you wonder why there is a model:

Dealer Quentin sells 1 part EUR/USD at cost 1.5000. He declares it on Twitter, expressing that the euro is relied upon to drop. That's it. Presently broker Tarantino pursues merchant Quentin on Twitter, and he sees the tweet. He knows dealer Quentin is a genius examiner, and he believes his judgment, so Tarantino opens a sell also. He made a stop loss of 30 pips and a focus of 60 pips dependent on his investigation.

A couple of hours after the fact, Tarantino's exchange hits the stop misfortune, and he understands adversity. On the following day, Tarantino awakens to see that the cost is at the 1.4000 level. One hundred pips drop! His companion Quentin has recognized a powerful benefit as of now. Why? Since Quentin utilized another methodology. He has his stop misfortune set at 1.5050.

This is how the gossip can be gainful for the individuals who start it and recognize what is happening and unfruitful for the individuals who indiscriminately pursue arbitrary explanations from to a great extent.

7. Stop framework jumping

Having a good time is something that I undoubtedly cherished before I turned into a dad of two. I'm sure you love it as well! Framework jumping then again is something that will explode your record. Quit pursuing dreams. It isn't the framework or methodology or strategy; it is you! Odds are you are the one that doesn't make it fill in as it should.

Each framework has its character. It resembles a pet. Your pooch doesn't talk; however, to figure out how to speak with that person, it requires some investment. You acclimate to one another. Your canine loves you. It is your closest companion. Allow it to change by your home. To make a propensity for setting off to the restroom outside. This is how you can make it work – with tolerance.

Give it time. Perceive how it functions. Get under its skin. Practice on the demo, gradually change to live. You will begin seeing fascinating realities that you didn't previously. It resembles perusing a book just because the second read is unique concerning the first, so it is the third one.

Attempt to adhere to one procedure for at any multi-rate month — four trading weeks. There's nothing more to it.

The Final Verdict

This primary hazard controlled system demonstrates that with a 55% success rate, and making more on victories than you lose on losing exchanges, it's conceivable to accomplish returns north of 20% every month with forex day exchanging. Most merchants shouldn't hope to make this much; while it sounds basic, as a general rule, it's increasingly troublesome.

With an OK win rate and hazard/compensate proportion, a devoted forex informal investor with an excellent technique can make somewhere in the range of 5% and 15% a month on account of influence. Likewise, recall, you needn't bother with a lot of money to begin; $500 to $1,000 is usually enough.

CHAPTER 7:

HOW TO START DAY TRADING WITH $500

Each new informal investor needs to begin someplace in the exchanging industry and to become active. You should have the correct data from the entire first day on the off chance that you need to become rich from doing this business. If you're on a restricted spending plan as a new dealer you can adapt just the rudiments and start day exchanging with $500 to get your exchanging business up and exchanging. When you are finished perusing the data in How to Start Day Trading With $500 you will be empowered.

The uplifting news is you don't have to know it all about day exchanging all at one time, nor might you be able to. The shockingly better news is that you don't need to figure out how today exchange each benefit class and how to turn into a specialist in each possible part of trading, you should focus on turning into an expert as opposed to being a generalist and How to Start Day Trading With $500 will help you to begin on your adventure to doing that.

To me, the start of the New Year should stamp the opportunity to set new objectives and drive yourself as far as possible. I attempted another little record.

This year I increased the stakes. I augmented my time allotment to a quarter of a year, increased my objective to $100,000, and sliced my beginning record to only $583.15. While my single expectation was, regardless of $700, the charge to open my career put me under $100 away from plunging beneath the base. I had a challenging situation to deal with.

It turned out, and I thought little of myself. I came to the $100k objective in about a month and a half, which even now stuns me. Here now, are the exercises I learned while achieving that.

1. THE HARDEST PART IS BEGINNING

This is valid for anything, not only day exchanging. However, no ifs, ands or buts, the first couple of weeks were the hardest. In that time, there were zero edges for the blunder, and my record was just barely above dipping under the base equalization. My fundamental apparatuses in this time were hotkeys, with the goal that I could get in and out of positions rapidly, and as much control as I could marshal.

My objective during this period was to catch around $0.20 of upside per exchange, and I tried to put hard stops if my position dropped by $0.10. To benefit as much as possible from these exchanges and to reduce commission expenses, I was managing a base measure of transactions, dealing with a great deal of volume, and depending on force to rapidly scalp breakouts before different merchants.

I discovered great accomplishment with this procedure since I held my desires under tight restraints. It was as yet troublesome, leaving endlessly with just $200 or $300 a day, although that was around 40 percent of my record. However, before the finish of my first week, I had dramatically increased my beginning equalization to about $1200.

2. EXPANDING EXCHANGES WHILE OVERSEEING HAZARD

That expanded record value truly helped speed things up in the next weeks. Just by having the option to make more exchanges and adequately scale my position, I had the opportunity to be progressively forceful. While I was as yet not out of the scope of totally failing the test, I dealt with my hazard adequately enough to limit potential and real misfortunes. I finished week two up by more than 600 percent and relentlessly developed that until I hit the $10k mark before finishing out January.

I was hoping to have a gigantic end to January. I completed my first $2,000 day on the last Friday of the month. The next Monday, I made barely short of $7,500, boosting my record above $22k. In any case, that achievement advanced beyond me, and the most recent day of January I wound up pursuing an exchange I realized I was past the point of no return on, I neglected to alter my position, and that cost me $6,000.

It was an unpleasant method to end the month, and it was my first misfortune on the year, yet I made up about $4,300 the following day was still poised to hit my first benchmark of $25k by mid-February. Incredibly, I would hit that sum and afterward much sooner than I initially suspected.

It was February 2 when I had a gigantic day for the test, just as a high-point for my profession as a merchant. I was as yet vexed about that $6k misfortune two days prior, and I was thus exchanging forcefully. While that conduct could have cost me more over the long haul, things, fortunately, broke the other path, and, in my little record alone, I made $14,800 in four exchanges, wrecking the $25k imprint and hitting $35k in a little more than a month. I made an extra $7,800 in my customary record. That $22k day remains my best exchanging day yet.

February kept on being incredible all through the month, where I would pick up somewhere in the range of $8,000-$10,000 before surrendering 70 to 80 percent of that the following day. In any case, my exactness was still around 67 percent, generally speaking. My benefits standardized close to the month's end, and I completed February picking up $60,000, getting my equalization to $69,000.

Walk, the last month began extremely solid. Indeed, it started so reliably that I had the option to hit the $100k objective inside the initial six days. It helped that I oversaw four long straight periods of outstanding additions, that solitary expanded, from $3,600, to $5,600, at that point $6,000, lastly peaking the objective with a colossal $8,800 day. By and large, I hit $100k from my measly $583 account in 44 days, which even now still stuns me.

3. NEVER DISMISS YOUR TECHNIQUE

The fundamental takeaway I got from experience was that having a procedure and staying with it is essential to discovering accomplishment as a dealer. There were times during the test where I was putting significant weight on myself to arrive at these objectives I had set, and on occasion, that pace neutralized me by convincing me to change my system and pursue exchanges.

I had this tension that I expected to keep causing rapid returns or make to awake for losing days that I would dismiss my methodology and end up not making as much as I could have on an exchange or in any event, winding up down because I was excessively forceful.

The best case of this is the days following when I hit my objective. In spite of the wonderful footing I had developed to that point, I completed the following day just up to $365. From that point forward, for four days in a row, I had a dark red streak in which I arrived at the midpoint of -$3.5k. I completed down almost $6,000 on the last day of that down streak. That was discouraging, yet it additionally indicated that I shouldn't seek after these enormous returns if they don't exist and understand when to cut my misfortunes as opposed to average down, which is never a brilliant thought.

I think those down days, following the accomplishment of my test, truly epitomizes why having an economic methodology and a level head will support your exchanging the long haul than hitting crazy returns. Odds are you will surrender a large portion of it in the following days by having a go at something dangerous than if you had quite recently adhered to what you knew works and accepting open doors as they show up.

QUICK GUIDE

Start with forex small scale parcels to learn. It's difficult to exchange whatever else with $500 effectively because commissions will gobble you up. When you have a predictable record for quite a long time ("at least" 3–6 months), you can discover approaches to get all the more subsidizing. I likewise prescribe swing exchanging, whether intraday or barely any days instead of scalping.

On a side note, realize that day exchanging won't make you productive overnight. It's a troublesome calling that takes a large number of hours to learn, to say the very least. Realize that considerably in the wake of spending those a great many hours, regardless, it probably won't be the profession for you. Some individuals still lose for quite a while, even though they've been doing it for a long time.

Try not to be tricked by con artists ready to give you "mystery sauce" or whatever for cash.

If you are not kidding, you need to begin with finding out about hazard the executives, cash the board, and so on first. If you aren't set up to work a great many hours, don't try the beginning.

DAY TRADING:

The strategy Bible to Invest in
Leveraging Options, Stocks, Forex,
and Making the Most of Market Swings.
The Ultimate Guide for Beginning Traders to
Build a Profitable Passive Income (Part 2)

By **James N. Miles**

Table of Contents

CHAPTER 8: DAY TRADING FOR A LIVING 107

STEP BY STEP INSTRUCTIONS TO MAKE A LIVING **112**

CHAPTER 9: DAY TRADING FOR DUMMIES 120

WHY DAY TRADING?..**123**

CHAPTER 10: GUIDE TO CRYPTO TRADING 130

CHAPTER 11: AVERAGE INCOME OF A DAY TRADER 144

A DAY TRADING STRATEGY IN REAL LIFE **154**

THE AMOUNT MONEY STOCK DAY TRADERS MAKE - FINAL WORD

....**157**

CHAPTER 12: DAY TRADING ACADEMIES 160

CHAPTER 13: DAY TRADING WEBSITES 164

CHAPTER 14: DAY TRADING DO'S AND DON'T'S..................182

CHAPTER 8:

DAY TRADING FOR A LIVING

Progressions in innovation have guaranteed anybody with a working web connection can begin day trading professionally. However, while it may be conceivable, how simple is it, and how on earth do you approach it? This section will look at the advantages of day trading professionally, what and where individuals are trading, and offer you some valuable hints.

IS DAY TRADING FOR A LIVING POSSIBLE?

The principal thing to note is right, bringing home the bacon on day trading is an impeccably suitable profession. However, it's not simpler or less work than customary daytime work. The advantages are fair that you work for yourself, and can design your work hours any way you need. Trading on a workstation additionally implies you can do it anyplace and anytime.

Be careful – there are many out there who guarantee to make a fortune on day trading; however, as a rule, these individuals are attempting to sell you something. Try not to accept the romotion or that there is such a thing as "pain-free income."

There are approaches to make it simpler, however – for instance, you don't have to make to such an extent if you live in (or move to) a minimal effort, low-charge nation. Reducing living expenses can likewise have a significant effect, as "bringing home the bacon" on something implies that salary covers costs.

ADVANTAGES VERSUS DRAWBACKS

Regardless of the trouble, there are some undeniable advantages to day trading professionally. To give some examples:

No boss – You're your very own boss. No more pandering to the requirements of requesting and preposterous managers. You can work precisely how you need it.

Hours – You set your very own working hours. In this day and age, there is always a market open. Thus, you can pick when you need to work and for how long, fitting it around different responsibilities. If you need a multi-week vacation, there's no HR office to visit first.

Overheads – No increasingly costly train pass to get the opportunity to work. No more petroleum and stopping costs.

No more expensive suits. You need a PC, a web connection, and some cash-flow to get moving.

Solace – while every other person is pressing their shirt for the day ahead, you can slip into some comfortable garments and start your 15-foot drive to your work area, with a crisp mug of espresso — not any more stuffy office or diverting partners to manage. You work from the comfort of your own home.

DISADVANTAGES

Regardless of the undeniable charms, remarks about day trading professionally additionally feature a few drawbacks. The most predominant are:

Lone way of life – Your associates may have driven you up the divider now and again, yet once in a while, it's good to have people around. Day trading professionally can get lonely. If you do not care for being without others, reconsider.

Conflicting compensation – Your pay will vary colossally. You may make $3,000 one day and lose $2,500 the next day. You most likely won't have a steady wage to depend on. What's more, if you take a vacation day, you won't get paid at all.

Profession movement – The main thing that can improve is your takings. You may likewise think that it's difficult to get back into the business world. Some time or another trading professionally discussions have proposed you'll be less employable by the end.

The fight against bots – Algorithms, robotized frameworks, and bots are on the whole assuming control over the market. They are currently answerable for a monstrous 60% of all market volume. While there will consistently be a spot for people in the market, you'll have to discover better approaches to adjust and develop if you need to keep up an edge.

WHAT ARE PEOPLE DAY TRADING?

One of the essential choices you'll make is what to begin day trading professionally. What are the prevalent protections and markets, among the individuals who day exchange professionally?

Stocks

Penny stocks

Forex

Cryptographic forms of money

Prospects

Eminis

CFDs

Items

Gold

Choices

Regardless of whether you're day trading penny stocks professionally or monetary forms, the instability and volume in your picked market will genuinely affect your potential benefits. The digital currency showcase, for instance, is exceptionally unstable, empowering some to bring home the bacon.

Though, day trading stocks professionally might be all the more testing. It is, as of now, an immersed market. Furthermore, a moderately high measure of beginning capital is required, and misfortunes could be all the more monetarily pulverizing.

Once more, day trading products or prospects professionally will show its difficulties.

TERRITORIAL DIFFERENCES

Regardless of whether you make it day trading as a living will likewise rely upon where you live, and the market you select. Day trading professionally in India, Indonesia or South Africa, offers unstable markets, yet you likewise have an extremely minimal cost of living, which makes "bringing home the bacon" progressively practical. Day trading professionally in the UK, US, Canada, or Singapore still offers a lot of chances, yet you have an abundance of rivalry to fight with, in addition to significant expenses of living. You won't be shy of instability or volume, yet you have to plunk down and compute the amount you should make by and large every week or month, just to survive.

Step by step instructions to Make A Living

Bringing home the bacon in day trading is no simple accomplishment. You'll have various costly obstructions to survive. Below the top tips have been grouped, to help keep you operating at a profit.

Arrangement

The question on many hopeful merchants' lips is, how to begin day trading professionally? The appropriate response is you need only a couple of essentials. Get those basics right, and you'll be in the most grounded situation to make a liberal compensation.

Equipment – You need a mid-extend PC and web connection. Any material or web accidents could cost you truly. Many propose having two screens ready for action, just in the event of crises.

Intermediary – Make sure you pick a broker that suits your needs. They have to offer aggressive costs, substantial client assistance, and simple to explore stage.

Methodology – You need a system that suits your trading style. It needs to depend on diagrams, examples, and specific pointers. It needs to empower you to make benefits on high volume, low-esteem exchanges.

Trading Office

This is a significant subject. Will you have a home office or attempt to exchange an assortment of regions on a workstation? You may have seen the pictures of a solitary dealer sitting behind six or even nine screens monitoring a wide range of information – however, is it essential? One option in contrast to attempting to commit some space at home to trading is to utilize leased work area space.

There is additional help that takes things a step further. ETrading HQ offers rented work area and office space, and additional day trading information and coordinated effort. Similarly, invested merchants can trade thoughts and methodologies up close and personal. The idea is growing in both London and New York and may make day trading significantly more reasonable for those worried about business sector information, isolation, and office space.

Capital

One of the first inquiries out of hopeful brokers' lips, is 'how much capital do you need?' The one prerequisite of day trading from home professionally is capital. Move back the shakers a couple of years, and you required at least $25,000 to begin day trading in the US. That, however, you generally needed to keep up at any rate that amount in your record.

These extreme guidelines implied that for most of the individuals, trading professionally was not monetarily achievable. Be that as it may, globalization of the budgetary business has enabled various stages to create outside of US guidelines. Today then you can begin with as little as $1,000 in your record.

How much capital you will need will rely upon what it is you need to begin trading.

Training

It is probably not possible to get the best odds of prevailing at day trading professionally. You have to use a broad scope of assets. Luckily, now you can discover free, instructive devices with only a couple of clicks of the mouse. The absolute best assets worth considering are:

Books – see our rundown of good reads, including available Google books.

Digital books – for example "New Trading Professionally Digital Book", by Alexander Elder (free download)

Audiobooks

Web journals

PDFs

Instructional exercise recordings

Gatherings – perfect for those hoping to begin making money in day trading stocks, fates, forex, and digital currencies.

Study guides

Digital recordings and MP3s

Flipkart

You'll discover guidance from experienced dealers on gatherings, websites, and chatrooms. You'll profit from point by point system models from books, PDFs, and instructional exercise recordings. A great deal of the day trading professionally digital books, epubs, and PDFs are accessible as free downloads as well and can be accessed through Kindle.

In case you're searching for explicit direction on the best way to make money in day trading forex, consider the forex page. Then again, see the stocks page in case you're keen on trading stocks from home professionally.

Hazard Management

In case you see how to do day trading professionally, one of the fundamental segments is how you deal with chance. As Larry Hite correctly declared, "All through my money related vocation, I have persistently seen instances of other individuals that I

have known being demolished by an inability to regard   chance.
It is on the off chance that you do not go out on a limb and take a hard look in danger, it will take you."

You need a framework that guarantees you have enough to make moves while holding enough capital that you don't need to return to regular everyday employment.

A decent framework rotates around stop-misfortunes and take-benefits. These enable you to prepare and counteract increased feelings assuming responsibility for choices.

Stop-misfortune – This is the cost at which you will sell a stock and take the loss.

It will destroy you hanging on with the expectation that it will return.

Take-benefit – This is the time when you will sell a stock and take the benefit. This will assist you in withholding that benefit by empowering you to sell before the time of combination kicks in.

Psychology

In case you're trading professionally, reliable and stable benefits are the objective, which will require a reliably taught personality. As Victor Sperandeo featured, "The way to progress is passionate order. If insight were the key, there would be significantly more individuals making cash trading."

It might sound clear now, however, when you have $2,500 hanging in the balance, and you've been gazing eagerly and rigidly at the screen throughout the previous six hours, keeping apprehension under control isn't so natural. A viable method to restrain your enthusiastic obligation is to utilize as much specialized assistance as could be expected. Holding your feelings in line will take practice, a lot of mix-ups, and afterward, significantly more errors. In any case, a perfect stunt that encourages numerous dealers is to concentrate on the exchange, not the cash. Take it from experienced merchant Alexander Elder, "The objective of an effective dealer is to make the best exchanges. Cash is optional."

End

The number of individuals day trading professionally since 2014 has skyrocketed. Is it sensible, however? The appropriate response is, it depends altogether on your aspiration and duty. It won't be a simple ride. Be what may, if it suits your working style, you pick the correct market, and you use the tips referenced; at that point, you could be one of only a handful to triumph.

CHAPTER 9:

DAY TRADING FOR DUMMIES

Figure out how to day trade online with our Day Trading for Dummies. There are six things each amateur should know before beginning day trading stocks. All that you have to think about day exchanging will be uncovered during this time exchanging for fledgling's aid.

On this day trading instructional exercise, we're going to allow you multi-day exchanging tips that will show you how today stock exchange works. Day trading is a real vocation that can give you a change from your customary 9 to 5 employment. We made this Day

Trading for Dummies manageable so you can maintain a strategic distance from the most widely recognized missteps amateur dealers will encounter.

We'll jump into day trading essentials, also, to further developed systems.

Day trading, which has been now explored in preceding sections, is the demonstration of purchasing and selling a monetary instrument inside a single trading day.

At whatever point you open trading to exploit little intraday value variances, and close that trading inside the same day day, you're occupied with day trading.

Entirely essential, isn't that so?

The main thing you need to remember is that if you close your situation before the market closes, you're an informal investor.

E.g., If you purchase and sell Bitcoin inside a single trading day, you are day trading Bitcoin.

Numerous active brokers use day trading procedures instead of lengthy haul trading methodologies. They are considered as probably the most ideal approaches to make easy money. Yet, we likewise need to remember the critical dangers that accompany day trading.

Choosing which style of trading is better, day trading, or long haul contributing boils down to something beyond your inclination. There are a few key variables, like mental control, and your capacity to act under strain. It's likewise imperative to recall that you can, at any time, fall flat if you don't have the correct methodology.

You might be asking yourself, "should I day exchange?" In the following section, we'll look at the attributes you have to turn into an active informal investor.

Who Should Day Trade?

Thinking about whether you should day trade? The best approach to make money in any market (stocks, Forex, products, cryptographic forms of money) is to discover an trading style that suits your character. A few people have an exclusive range of abilities that is more appropriate for day trading than others.

Turning into a fruitful informal investor requires something beyond a decent day trading methodology. You likewise must have:

Mental discipline.

Snappy thinking capacities.

The capacity to work under enormous pressure.

If your character doesn't coordinate your trading style, you can wind up in an unsafe circumstance. For instance, if your trading style is to move at a slower pace, you may not be appropriate for day trading. You will be more qualified to swing trading.

Fundamentally, you have to understand your trading period character.

Veteran exchanging therapist and a smash hit creator, Brett Steenbarger, found that trading achievement implies concentrating on your character qualities.

Something else to recall is that day exchanging additionally has administrative implications. FINRA will enable you to take part in this trading if you have at least $25,000 in your account. This is otherwise called the PDT rule (Pattern Day Trading). Things being what they are, would it be advisable for you to attempt day trading?

If you have more than $25,000 in your account and work well under strain, day trading can be a decent choice. It relies upon your trading character, chance resilience, and monetary liquidity. If you're fortunate, you fill in every one of the necessities in this area. You're one step nearer making a vocation as an informal investor. Presently, you have to gain proficiency with the correct method to day trade. For those of you who don't meet the necessities or would prefer not to change your retirement or investment funds, you can generally utilize a social trading stage to duplicate an expert informal investor.

Why Day Trading?

All in all, what are the advantages of day trading?

- No medium-term danger of holding the stock.
- You can profit both when the stock cost is rising and when the stock cost is falling.
- You can utilize an extra edge. The utilization of use and quick market passage and ways out make day exchanging stocks appealing.
- You don't need to perform rigorous research about the organization's basics. You are just theorizing on the typical value vacillation.
- You can make cash immediately contrasted with long haul exchanging.

These are only a couple of the favorable circumstances that day trading brings to the table. This ought to rouse you why day trading is a decent way to deal with trading the money related markets. You may likewise be keen on our guide on day trading ETFs.

Next, we figure out how to day trade stocks in a way that will give you consistency.

In case you're keen on day exchanging professionally, this 3 stage procedure will show you how to day trade stocks with progress.

STEP BY STEP INSTRUCTIONS TO DAY TRADE STOCKS

Figuring out how to day trade includes something beyond picking the most significant day trading stocks. It requires an arrangement of planning, practice, and persistence. Here are some central standards you have to pursue when beginning with day trading.

DEPEND ON THE "THREE P'S" RULE:

Planning – You have to build up your very own triumphant day trading plan, else, you might come up short. It's essential to have an individual guide for your trades because there are numerous tempests you can encounter when trading.

Practice – A fundamental bit of your exchanging toolbox ought to be to rehearse your procedure until you ace the round of day trading. Redundancy is the mother of all learning.

Persistence – Once you have your exchanging plan prepared, have the tolerance to adhere to your guidelines.

You have to know when to day trade, what time to trade, which day trading stocks are the best to handle, and which day trading methodologies to utilize.

If you ace the specialty of tolerance and adhere to your day trading rules, it very well may be a genuine distinct advantage for your trading.

If you need to improve your prosperity rate and further enhance your methodology, you have to know the best occasions to day trade.

BEST TIMES FOR DAY TRADING

Things being what they are, what is the best time for day exchanging? The best occasions for day exchanging are during the first and the last standard market exchanging hours, between 9:30 - 10:30 AM EST and 3:00 - 4:00 PM EST.

The financial exchange tends to create the majority of its value developments during explicit occasions of the day.

It's well-known that the securities exchange is the most unpredictable during the first hour of the exchanging day (9:30 – 10:30 AM EST) and the last hour of standard market exchanging (3:00 – 4:00 PM EST). The experts frequently

allude to these as the power hour.

A day exchanging procedure can't get by without instability. Unpredictability is the life and breath of any fruitful informal investor.

Presently, you have the outlook of a determined marksman prepared to hang tight for the best-exchanging chances quietly.

There's one more thing left for you to finish your training about day trading.

If you need to carry your game to the next level and approach day trading the correct way, you'll have to figure out how to day trade stocks utilizing a graph.

Value Action and Chart Patterns

Day trading methodologies ordinarily depend on two kinds of stock examination: basic and specialized investigation.

To discover potential day trading openings, you have to concentrate on an outline based specialized investigation. You need to have one excellent value activity design that rehashes each day to have accomplished as an informal investor.

If your preferred stock will, in general, produce a similar example after some time, the odds are that stock will keep on going in the same direction. That is the reason we prescribe concentrating verifiable stock graphs to discover dull models.

At the point when you scan for a day trading design search for perfect and simple value activity.

In case you're making some hard choices, deciding if there is an example on the stock diagram or not, odds are this is certifiably not a tradable stock example. You have to search for unsurprising and solid stock outline examples to be a fruitful informal investor. For instance, breakouts that happen during the primary hour of regular exchanging hours, and are joined by expanded volume, have a high likelihood of seeing the finish. The ideal approach today exchange breakouts are to hang tight for a nearby over the obstruction level. You'll likewise need to see a nearby underneath the help level before you short sell the stock. Day trading breakouts is a simple and clear example that exploits the instability produced by the break of these critical levels. This is a decent strategy to figure out how to day trade stocks and develop your record.

Last Words

Day trading requires serious core interest. If you figure out how to day exchange the correct way, you can achieve budgetary autonomy. When you make a beneficial exchanging plan, you'll have the option to spot monotonous and gainful stock outline designs. If you need assistance, you can achieve the entirety of the above through our exchanging assets and exchanging systems that are so famous here on the TSG site.

Before you build up your day exchanging methodologies, ensure you have each point secured through this article before you hazard any of your well-deserved cash. With the S&P 500 arriving at new untouched highs consistently, there will never have been a superior time to begin day exchanging stocks professionally.

CHAPTER 10:

GUIDE TO CRYPTO TRADING

In the preceding section, I expounded on getting digital currencies and what to search for when contributing just as getting purchase/sell dividers on trades. This still leaves the question, what would be a good idea for me to search for while picking a coin to day trade?

Presently I have to stop things here and state, I am not a certified monetary consultant. The data below are my exercises, perceptions, and involvement with the crypto world that I need to pass on. If you choose to put resources into digital money, contribute what you are eager to lose. Do your very own examination and gain from the same number of individuals as you can to get a balanced comprehension of digital currency trading.

You should have a hard spine to deal with the unpredictability of this market.

I've lost a massive number of dollars in hours. However, by holding and remaining solid, it returns.

Because of this unpredictability of the crypto world, you can make money off practically any coin available if you have enough understanding. In any case, even I don't have that measure of experience required. In that capacity, I'll be handling exchanging coins with a lower chance included and how to guarantee you can generally make some money.

REASON

The principal activity, which I additionally mentioned in my past chapters, is to make sense of what your objective is for day trading? Is it to earn 5 percent benefits each month and have a little hazard, or is it to double your cash every month and giggle even with a chance? Or then again, perhaps it is to develop a decent base to begin spreading your portfolio into different coins? Despite the explanation, it is essential to recognize it and remember it. This will provide you guidance and a sound base for your necessary leadership. Without it, you will wind up drifting in the vast sea of value developments, being thumped forward and backward by each ascent and plunge. You need a stay point, and this will be your motivation.

When you have clarified your objectives in day exchanging, I would likewise propose you make sense of how quickly you need to arrive (if you haven't as of now). This will help in deciding your hazard profile. If you need to double your cash in multi-week (Probably somewhat unreasonable) at that point, you can toss hazard out the window and go insane with your trades. It probably won't be excessively profitable, yet if you need a gradual benefit increment, you can unwind and settle in for an okay coin with generally safe exchanges.

TRADE

One of the main things to search for after choosing your motivation, even before you have selected your coin, is to settle on a trade you need to utilize. There would be three fundamental perspectives that you need to think about when picking a deal.

First, guarantee it has a wide assortment of well-known coins and has high exchanging volume. This ensures there will be adequate movement on the trade for exchanging purposes. A regularly entrenched trade ought to exchange in

any event $200M at any rate. In a perfect world, you would look at one who has $0.5M–$1M exchanging volume like clockwork. I, at present, do my trading with Binance, which has exchanged $1.9M over the most recent 24 hours and has nearly 250 distinctive exchanging sets.

The next thing to look at with trade is the exchanging charges. Some of the time, trades will have various charges with various criteria for a similar trade. For instance, with Binance they have a 0.1 percent charge for exchanges if you pay with the neighborhood coin being exchanged; however in the event that you spend with Binance Coins, at that point they will cancel a large portion of the expenses for the primary year, bringing about just 0.05 percent charges per exchange. Different trades will frequently shift the costs if you are a 'producer' or 'taker.' A 'producer' is somebody who places in an exchange demand that isn't satisfied straightaway. Subsequently, they are 'making' some portion of the purchase/sell orders. A 'taker' is somebody who is placing in an exchange demand that is satisfying another person's exchange request; henceforth, you are 'removing' ceaselessly one of the purchase/sell orders. Frequently the expenses are higher for 'takers' contrasted with 'producers.' When taking a gander at costs of 0.1 percent, 0.25 percent, 0.5 percent, and so on, you may think this is minuscule and doesn't generally make a difference. I can't emphasize enough that it does make a difference if you plan on doing long haul exchanging. It is on the slim chance that you are a beneficial broker beginning with $100 and make 2.5 percent benefit a day, and we exacerbate this more than one year of exchanging, at that point paying 0.5 percent charges every day accepting you do one exchange a day will decrease your benefit by a considerable number of dollars. This sounds insane; however you crunch the numbers, it turns out the equivalent. Make sense of how frequently you will do exchanges, for example, every day, bi-day by day, week by week, and so forth and work out which technique on which trade will lessen your expenses to an acceptable level.

The third thing to look at is that it is so natural to pull back assets from this specific trade. Check charges, criteria, confirmation, limits, and so on. When you have made benefits, you will need to have the option to pull them back without having issues or paying a lot of it in expenses.

THE COIN

The next thing I would recommend you look at is the cost of the coin and trading volume. These angles are high to look at independently just as together. The price can be identified with your hazard profile. I state this freely, yet it is a little pointer. As a rule, if a coin is modest, at that point, there could be more hazards required for two reasons. Right off the bat, the low cost could be a sign of little network trust or unfortunate venture the board/correspondence. This makes a small request and therefore brings down the estimation of the coin. The subsequent explanation is that if a coin is esteemed at $0.02 and it drops by just
1 cent, then your speculation will be sliced in half only like that.

I'm not saying don't put resources into modest coins, yet know that there are more dangers included. On the other side, there are more benefits included. If you purchase at $0.01, you need a 1 cent rise to double your cash.

Concerning the trading volume of a coin, the idea is like that of trade. You need something that everybody is purchasing/selling as it shows a level of network certainty, just as liquidity—the capacity to understand your benefits rapidly or move them into cash you can utilize.

One perspective NOT to get tricked with is by observing a coin with a high trading volume, yet then you see it is genuinely costly and think it isn't fluid. For instance, a coin has an trading amount of $1,000,000. However, you know, it costs $1,000 per coin. This implies just 1000 coins are traded over the 24hr period. Contrast this with a coin with a similar trading volume yet a coin cost of $1, meaning 1,000,000 coins are trading each day. This ought not to influence your choice necessarily because the sum you will exchange remains the equivalent in $ cost, not in the number of coins. Your $100 in the precious currency, is still just worth $100 in the modest coin. I'm as of now exchanging KNC/ETH which has an exchanging volume of $1.7M and a cost of $3.75.

When you have a bunch of coins limited presently dependent on the above criteria (obviously ensure the coin is traded on your chose trade in the exchanging pair you need) at that point, the time has come to begin looking at things in more fine-grained detail. This is the place you look at the venture itself, the age of the coin, the group behind it, the network commitment, and so forth. This causes you to understand the life span of the coin and if the coin's general worth is probably going to rise. Seeing what is known as the 'Guide' of a coin ordinarily will recognize key dates along a course of events in which venture updates or discharges will happen. These can be great occasions to hold instead of trade as these can knock the cost up a piece. In any case, recollect each unexpected cost increment is regularly due for a 'remedy' I will go into this more in a later article.

Examples

Since we have a coin chosen, we can begin watching the exchanging designs. I would say you look at this for half a month to see how it responds to specific occasions of the day and week, and how it responds to news and so forth.

This will assist you with boosting your trades and reduce the sudden misfortunes from awful transactions which are unsurprising.

For instance, with the KNC/ETH pair, there is frequently decisive action at 9 am, and 7 pm AEST and regularly Sunday/Monday have a weak response. Likewise, when there are enormous declarations made by KNC on Twitter, it takes around 15-20 minutes before the market responds. I won't give proof of this because there is an excessive amount to go into in this article. However, this should give you a thought of the kind of examples you are searching for. On the slim chance that the coin is generally new, at that point, there will be more subtle examples contrasted with a more established coin.

If you have been engaged with exchanging either stock, fiat monetary standards, or digital currencies, then you may have run over the term 'purchase divider' or 'sell divider.' Tossing it in a sentence positively makes you look shrewd, yet what does it mean? Also, in what capacity can this information be used by individuals like you and me — the essential broker?

To address these inquiries, we'll have to take a step back and see what purchase/sell orders are first. At the point when you need to buy a few coins, it isn't as basic as setting up a record on trade and paying the coins off the association. The deal is only an office in which two clients can meet to swap resources. You need to purchase their coins with another coin of significant worth (typically ETH or BTC), they need to sell their coins and get BTC or ETH in return. At the point when you agree on a value, the exchange is made, and each client's wallets change to reflect the consummation of the trade. Presently this sounds exceptionally muddled and repetitive.

Furthermore, it would be if you needed to do everything. However, you don't. You should place in a solicitation, choosing the coin, the sum, and the value per coin. This is known as a purchase request. Precisely the same happens for those that need to sell. However, this is known as a sell request.

Ordinarily, these will be set as rundown until dropped — which implies it will remain as an unfilled request until it is possible that it gets filled or you lose it. Presently you can envision a large number of individuals putting the purchase and sell arranges on the trade, making a bunch of requests. The trade at that point coordinates any up that cover naturally. The rest are recorded freely until filled or dropped.

Since all requests that are covering are consequently satisfied, it makes it simple to set and overlook until your request gets filled. Some of the time, for an enormous purchase (or sell) request, it may take different smaller applications to top it off, this may mean you will see your request incompletely filled, at that point somewhat more, until it gets filled. Presently, innately, there will consistently be a hole between the most elevated purchase request and the least sell request. This hole is basically where the present coin's cost will sit. Typically, it will be the last finished request cost. This is how the market can drive up or down the coin's price.

When there is a considerable purchase request, then the green heap will rise vertically rather than in little augmentations. It appears to be like an enormous advance — or a divider! This means if there is a considerable purchase request of 10,000 coins at 0.003 ETH when most of the sell orders are just 10's or 100's of coins, then it will be hard to satisfy this request. If this request can't be filled, at that point, it implies no demands beneath this divider cost will be satisfied, basically preventing the cost from going underneath the divider. Something very similar happens when there is a sell divider.

Presently, when a purchase divider is set up, everybody who has a request underneath this realizes their request will be probably not be filled, AND anybody hoping to purchase rapidly likewise realizes they should put their purchase request at a more significant expense than the divider, guaranteeing it will get filled first. This will, at the point, drive the cost up to as the individuals would then be able to begin putting sell arranges in at more significant expenses excessively because of the fortuitous interest. A sell divider will have the contrary impact, bringing down the cost.

Foundation Tad on these dividers.

A portion of these dividers are real, and it just implies that many individuals or one individual with a great deal of cash accepts that at that specific value, it is the correct choice to buy, yet now and then these dividers are endeavors at value control.

Somebody who holds an enormous level of the piece of the pie of a coin is known as a whale — they are the massive fish in the ocean, they cause a sprinkle. So, when a whale has enough assets to put a considerable purchase request in, they can without any assistance making a purchase divider. They would do this to attempt to control the market, making counterfeit publicity. I state counterfeit, as they never mean to purchase this numerous amount of coins at this significant expense. However, they may effectively possess a few coins they obtained at a lower cost. By putting this 'phony' purchase request in, they would like to drive the price up, at that point, enabling them to sell their presently possessed coins for a social benefit. This enormous dump of coins will, at that point, cause the market to understand the phony publicity and bring the value way down. This enables the whale to buy more coins with the benefits they have quite recently made. Here and there things don't generally go as arranged. If the purchase divider doesn't control the cost to go higher, at that point, the whale will drop the huge request if the price gets too low where their application may begin to get filled. This can have the contrary influence, which could make the value drop as individuals accept this enormous request has been filled and everybody needs to sell before the value drops further. This could even have been the whale's arrangement from the beginning to get some modest coins.

What I'm attempting to show is that a phony purchase divider may be set up to drive the cost up or down. This is the reason it is something that you can't utilize alone to direct your exchange decisions. Taking this guidance, there is one thing to look for with these. If you put in a request just underneath a purchase request or directly over a sell request may mean you pass up some benefit. The purpose behind this is if the purchase divider is fruitful in driving the cost up/holding it steady. At that point your request will never get satisfied; consequently you could have included by merely pushing your purchase request cost up just a couple of focuses with the goal that it is either equivalent to or marginally over the divider. On the opposite end, however, if the purchase divider is (fruitful) in pushing the cost down when it is evacuated, then the price will probably descend various focuses. Hence your request will be filled. However, it would likewise have been filled if you had brought down the purchase request's cost down further.

These dividers may appear to be very strong and steadfast, in any event, defying now and again. In any case, if you see a purchase/sell divider, ensure you watch out for it as they can be dropped and reset inside seconds. You will frequently observe them going here and there in light of the present cost.

For instance, suppose I need to drive the cost up from $1.00 to $1.20 instead of holding it consistent or dropping it. I will set my purchase divider at $0.99, which will drive others to put their requests over this value, say spread from $1.00 to $1.05. I reset my purchase divider at $1.04, again powering others to put their requests over this value, spreading from $1.05 to $1.10. I proceed again until the cost comes to $1.20 and afterward settled in various medium sell arranges not to disturb the significant expense, yet enabling me to sell my coins.

At that point, put more significant sell requests and force my purchase request off totally when I'm prepared for the cost to drop once more. Then, I can begin the procedure once more.

Regardless of whether you do the first day trading and these dividers are one of only a handful of things you search for to help with your request position, you will show improvement over the chance that you overlook them. Adding this to a couple of other fundamental exchanging standards, and you will make sure to begin building a few benefits as this unstable coin development is a broker's heaven.

CHAPTER 11:

AVERAGE INCOME OF A DAY TRADER

I magine a scenario where I revealed to you that while trading salary has numerous factors. But, by applying some essential research strategies, you can go to a reliable gauge of what an informal investor can make dependent on their area, beginning capital, and business status.

In this section, I am going to share various sources that can give you clear gauges to use to decide your potential benefit potential.

Let's face it, a significant number of people are thinking about going out without anyone else and are not hoping to find a new line of work.

Anybody that tells you a conclusive range for a day trading pay is pulling your leg.

I may as well be talking with one of my children about Yo Gabba (one of their preferred shows on Nickelodeon).

Presently, for all you corporate individuals that can go to destinations like vault.com or talk with your insider companions to check the amount you can make in an trading work, don't anticipate hard numbers from any of these sources.

The reason being, there is a large group of outside variables that play into how a much cash you can make. In this article, we will get down to cold hard certainties. Sit back, unwind, and get some espresso.

A DECISION YOU SHOULD NOT TAKE LIGHTLY

Do not trifle with this choice, and you should gauge the upsides and downsides. First of all, trading for another person will permit you the chance to use the devices and systems of an outfit that is ideally beneficial.

Some of the positives of trading for another person is evaluating the weights of distinguishing both a triumphant framework and a tutor that can help you en route.

If you are not beneficial "enough," be set up to have a more significant number of rules tossed at you than when you were in sixth grade.

This degree of administration over your trading action is because of the reality you are utilizing another person's cash, so profit or become used to somebody revealing to you how to relax.

The one significant upside for day trading for another person is you will get paid. This pay is likely insufficient to live on; however, you do get a check.

At the point when you go out alone, there is no pay. You are a financial specialist wanting to make payments. We will go into this theme a lot further. Later on, however, I need to ensure I express this forthright.

LICENSES

On the slim chance that you choose to work for the firm and are exchanging customer's cash or conceivably interfacing with clients, you will require your Series 7 and perhaps your Series 63 permit.

SERIES 7

The Series 7 will give you the permit to trade. Last I checked, the test cost $305 and relying upon the outfit will be secured by the firm.

SERIES 63

The Series 63 is the test you should take after the Series 7. This test licenses you to request orders for stock inside a point of view state. A straightforward perspective about this is that the 7 gives you the privilege to trade on a government level, and the 63 enables you to work inside the limits of state laws.

I don't anticipate covering the theme of day exchanging for somebody finally because I haven't lived it.

From what I do know, you are required to finish some in-house preparation programs for the firm you speak to. For venture houses, you will get a decent base pay, enough to keep you at the lower white-collar class for New York.

NEED TO KNOW THE BEST PART?

Your base stock merchant pay could go from 50,000 - 70,000 dollars US, which is only enough for you to take care of your link tab, feed yourself and perhaps take a taxi or two. In any case, this does not cover meals, vehicles, excursions, tuition-based schools, and so on.

In this way, you can rapidly see that for you to be successful, you're going to need to make your reward. There is only one catch; you need to profit at day trading. Superficially, this sounds sensible because you bring down your hazard profile by having another pay stream of a base compensation; in any case, you need to perform to remain utilized, and will just get around 10-30 percent of the benefits you get from your exchanging movement.

In light of these numbers, you would need to make about 300k in trading benefits to break 100k in compensation.

Most likely, the advantage of trading with an organization is, after some time, your purchasing influence will rise, and you have none of the drawbacks since it's the organization's cash. The key is ensuring you have a lot of money under administration.

As should be evident in the infographic over, the way to making genuine cash is to begin dealing with different assets. You, in one way or another, draw that off, and you will make by and large 576k per year.

Indeed you read that right.

I realize the 576k looks engaging; however, recall it is purely hard labor to get to the highest point of the mountain.

The other thing from the infographic is that the usual reward is beginning to drift higher, and if things go as conjecture will surpass the downturn top not long from now.

Along these lines, if one of your objectives is to profit, you are looking in the right business.

REGULAR INCOME TRADING FOR A COMPANY

The widely appealing individual can hope to make somewhere in the range of 100k and 175k. In conclusion, if you are below normal, hope to get a pink slip.

In any case, pause - there's more.

Certainly, if we broaden our exploration past New York, you will see the regular pay for a "Merchant" is $89,496.

Try not to trust me?

OPEN TRADING FIRMS

Be that as it may, I can consider many jobs where you can make near $89k, and it doesn't require the degree of responsibility and hazard taking required for trading.

You might be thinking, "this person just revealed to me it could go as high as $250k to $500k in case I'm better than expected, where does $89k become an integral factor."

What I have talked about so far are the pay rates for trading on an open market organization. Good karma attempting to get precise information from the first-class universe of private value brokers. What you will discover is regularly the top brokers from Chase and Bank of America endeavor out to flexible investments, as a result of the opportunity in their exchanging choices and the more significant compensation potential. Here's the most significant part, with the general population firms, corporate objectives will frequently drive a segment of your other targets.

The magnificence of the multifaceted investment world is while there are still organization objectives, you have the chance to eat a more significant amount of what you slaughter. It's nothing for a top broker to out-acquire their chief if they carry enough of an incentive to the firm.

What amount do you figure you could make?

ADVANTAGES OF DAY TRADING FOR AN ORGANIZATION

1. Pay
2. Medical advantages
3. The renown of working for a venture bank or fence investments
4. No danger of individual capital
5. Climb the corporate positions to deal with various assets
6. A drawback of day trading for an organization
7. Must connect with customers
8. Office legislative issues
9. By and large, you get 20% of benefits (Public Firm)

DAY TRADING FOR A PROP FIRM

Day trading for prop firms can feel similar to living on the edge.

Like trading for an organization, you will get some preparation before the prop firm enables you to trade with their cash and approach their frameworks. From that point forward, all likenesses between exchanging for a prop firm and an organization contrast.

Try not to expect any human services of paid downtime. You won't have a base compensation or yearly audits. The prop firms will expect you to store cash to begin utilizing their foundation.

The advantages are the prop firm will part benefits with you anywhere from a third and up to half. The drawbacks are again no compensation, and you bear a portion of the torment with regards to misfortunes.

However, here's the rub, the explanation prop firm merchants make not precisely those for the speculation houses is access to capital. Since you are likely trading the exclusive firm proprietor's cash, the pool of assets you approach is constrained.

I would state a better than an expected broker for a prop firm can make about 150k to 250k every year. The typical broker will do somewhere in the range of 60k and 100k, and underperformers will have such huge numbers of position limits set for them, they are fundamentally rehearsing and not profiting. These underperformers will probably expel themselves from the game because rehearsing doesn't take care of the bills.

ADVANTAGES
- Split benefits with Prop Firm
- Low commission rates
- No Boss
- Increment Margin

NEGATIVES
- Utilize your cash-flow to begin
- Loss of individual riches
- Constrained preparing
- No medical advantages or paid downtime
- No vocation movement
- Just cause cash off what you to acquire

DAY TRADING SALARIES STATE BY STATE IN US

Notwithstanding the information showed in the infographic from the Office of the New York State Comptroller, I need to take it a step further to distinguish the beginning pay for a passage level exchanging work the country over.

I chose passage level to give a counter to the middle national normal of $89k for trading work. Keep in mind that $89k is a normal of junior trading employments - right to the most senior.

Along these lines, in the situation that you are genuinely beginning and are offered $50k, don't get disheartened. We need to start someplace!

True to form, the New England and Pacific districts of the nation have the most significant pay. Presently, these can be just ascribed to the standard average cost for essential items. However, you can check your state to see what you can hope to make as a lesser dealer.

The Myth

A large number of the online articles are explicit about the benefit proportion you can expect when you become an informal investor. For instance, an article by Cory Mitchell that shows up on the Vantage Point Trading site spreads it out in detail and expect to start exchanging capital of $30,000:

"Accept your normal five exchanges for every day, so if you have 20 exchanging days a month, you make

100 exchanges for every month. You make $3,750, however despite everything you have commissions and perhaps some different charges. Your expense per exchange is $5/contract (full circle). Your bonus costs are: 100 exchanges x $5 x 2 agreements = $1000."

In Mitchell's model, your net after bonuses is $2,750. Since you began with $30,000, that is a month to month return of a little more than 9 percent. If you reinvest those benefits on a month to month premise, toward the end of one year, you'll have an interest of $55,944 and change. Not awful, and the best news is, you don't have to get dressed for work.

The Reality

Here's a sure sign that the truth might be very not quite the same as the legend.

As indicated by a 2013 investigation of the Taiwanese securities exchange drove by business analyst Brad Barber of the University of California, Davis, Graduate School of Management, and including the ordinary trade that market over 14 years, under 1 percent of all member dealers made money. Putting it another way, 99 percent of the informal investors lost cash.

Another concentrate by Barber and individual UC financial analyst Terrance Odean dissected the market returns of more than 66,000 U.S. families exchanging the U.S. securities exchange over a five-year time frame from 1991 to 1996. They reasoned that continuous dealers (not informal investors, mainly, however, including casual investors and the individuals who exchange stocks as often as possible) failed to meet expectations of financial specialists who utilized a purchase and hold methodology by about a third. The more often a given member traded, the more they failed to meet expectations of the average return.

A 2013 research study from the Cass Business School at the City University of London, reasoned that monkeys tossing darts at the stock pages could accomplish preferable outcomes over stock merchants. Alright, they were carefully reenacted monkeys, yet at the same time...

To give you a superior thought of your odds as a "proficient" informal investor, think about the North American Securities Administrators Association records trading courses – the web-based "trading schools" that show you how to prevail as an informal investor – as a best 10 risk to financial specialists, alongside Ponzi plans and obscure exchanging calculations dependent on Fibonacci numbers.

A Day Trading Strategy in real life

Accept a day exchanging system where the stop misfortune is $0.04, and your objective is $0.06.

Your account balance is $30,000, so the most hazard per trade is $300. With a $0.04 stop misfortune, you can take 7,500 ($300/$0.04) shares on each trade and remain inside your $300 chance top (excluding commissions).

If it's not too much issue, take note that to receive 7,500 offers, the offer cost should be under $16 (achieved by $120,000 in purchasing power divided by 7,500 proposals). If the per-share price is more than $16 you'll have to take fewer offers. The stock additionally needs to have enough volume for you to make such a position (see Look for These Qualities in a Day Trading Stock).

Working with this procedure, here's a case of the amount you might make day trading stocks:

55 exchanges were victories/profitable: 55 x $0.06 x 7,500 shares = $24,750

45 exchanges were losses: 45 x - $0.04 x 7500 shares = ($13,500)

Your gross benefit would be $24,750 - $13,500 = $11,250.

Your net benefit, which incorporates the expense of commissions, is $11,250 - commissions ($30 x 100 = $3,000) = $8,250 for the month.

This is the hypothetical benefit, and a few elements can and will lessen your interests; see Refinements below to see how this number gets balanced for this present reality.

The reward to chance proportion of 1.5 is used because it is genuinely traditionalist and intelligent of the open doors that happen throughout the day, consistently in the financial exchange.

The beginning capital of $30,000 is additionally a surmised equalization to begin day trading stocks; more is prescribed if you wish to trade more costly stocks.

The $0.04 stop and $0.06 are utilized similarly, for instance. Contingent upon the unpredictability of the stock, this may be diminished, yet more than likely extended if the stock moves a lot. As the stop continues, you'll have to lessen the number of offers taken to keep up a similar degree of hazard insurance.

Refinements to Your Strategy

Frequently on winning trades, it won't be possible to get every one of the offers you need; the value moves too rapidly. In this way, accept on winning exchanges you end up with, by and large, 6,000 offers. This diminishes the net benefit to $3,300, rather than $8,250.

Little modifications can affect profit.

Some different presumptions were likewise made in the model above. Chiefly that the dealer can locate a stock that enables them to ultimately use their capital (counting influence) while utilizing a 1.5 reward-to-hazard proportion, discovering five trades a day will be more troublesome on certain days than others (seee How to Find Volatile Stocks for Day Trading).

Value slippage is additionally a particular piece of trading. That is the point at which a more significant misfortune happens than anticipated, when utilizing a stop misfortune. Slippage will, to a great extent, rely upon the volume of the stock comparative with your position size.

To represent slippage, decrease your net profit figures by 10 percent. Given this situation and refinements, it is conceivable to make about $2,970, exchanging a $30,000 account (the $3,300 referenced above, diminished by 10 percent).

Modify this situation in a like manner dependent on your stop and target (standard reward to chance), capital, slippage, win rate, standard win/misfortune position sizes, and commissions. Given your proposed methodology, it is conceivable to inquire about quite a bit of this before you start trading to understand the amount you can make.

The amount Money Stock Day Traders Make - Final Word

The above situation demonstrates it is possible to make more than 20 percent for every month with day trading, hypothetically. This is high by regular measures. Most brokers ought not to hope to make this when representing exact issues, like slippage and not continually having the option to get the full position they want on winning trades.

With a 55 percent win rate and with a procedure that produces more significant victories than failures, making 5 percent to 15 percent+ every month is conceivable. However, it isn't simple, even though the numbers make it look that way. These figures speak to what is feasible for those that become fruitful day trading stocks; recall, however, day exchanging has a low achievement rate, particularly among guys.

CHAPTER 12:

DAY TRADING ACADEMIES

Regardless of whether you're new to the game, or you're a veteran hoping to coordinate with different masters, day-trading schools can conceivably give you what you need to succeed. However, regardless of whether they're online courses, individual counsels, or gathering sessions, not all the day trading schools are the same.

They can fluctuate broadly, both in cost and in quality.

KEY TAKEAWAYS

There are plenty of day-trading schools that show the instruments for progress.

Every certified school should assist students with building up a sharp understanding of the business sectors they wish to day trade, methodologies to assist them with boosting benefits, coaching figures, and help after the classes have finished.

Day-trading foundations can concentrate on various markets, including values, fates, and outside trade.

PICKING A DAY-TRADING SCHOOL: THE 3 ELEMENTS

High day-trading schools should highlight the following three key components:

Establishment. This alludes to a sharp understanding of the market you wish to day trade, just as methodologies to assist you with augmenting benefits. Such data is accessible from online stock trading, choices trading, or fates trading courses, just as from reading the material - frequently for little or no cost. Numerous day-trading schools even reveal their central methodologies for nothing, as a temptation to take their paid classes.

Coaching. To make day-trading progress, it is fundamental to acknowledge essential input from onlookers who can more readily assess your trading style.
It's difficult to self-break down your day-trading execution. The same way that

it takes an outsider to assess your golf swing, it takes the sharp eye of a tutor, to recognize and address your day-trading imperfections.

Proceeding with Support. It's conceivable to create post-graduation unfortunate propensities; it's essential to keep up a robust system of supporters to hold you under tight restraints. Much the same as competitors, proficient brokers may encounter droops that can send them into a descending spiral, without outside help set up, to assist them with coursing right.

Trading Academy Cost

The web-based exchanging foundation educational cost will differ upon the program or course that you'll choose to get the hang of trading. Be that as it may, each one of the courses is intended to help you turn into a super dealer.

CHAPTER 13:

DAY TRADING WEBSITES

1. SidewaysMarkets.com | Futures Trading Education Blog -- Los Angeles

About Blog; SchoolOfTrade.com day trading training and systems for Crude Oil, Gold, E-smaller than expected Futures. Prepared to be a Professional Day Trader? Our people group of informal investors, swing brokers, and hawkers exhibit how to win benefits that the vast majority dream of viably.

Around three posts for each month.

Since Feb 2009

2. Day Trading Academy - Investing and Day Trading Education

Day Trading Academy - Investing and Day Trading EducationAbout Blog Day Trading Academy's Blog Here at Day Trading Academy (DTA), we give an unparalleled investigation of the worldwide speculation markets and potential changes. Pursue this blog to get showcase driving day trading training, trading instructing, and contributing organization offering a genuine way of turning into an expert informal investor.

Around one post for every month.

Since Aug 2011

3. Warrior Trading | Day Trading Education Blog

Vermont, USA

About Blog; Warrior Trading shows understudies how to Day Trade Momentum Strategies. We audit our trades every day for understudies in our Chat Room. Warrior Trading is the quickest developing network of dealers on the web. We train the Warrior Trading methodologies. Pursue this blog to figure out how to Day Trade!

Around four posts every week.

Since Jun 2014

4. LiveStream Trading

About Blog; Stock Trading Chat and Screen Share. LiveStream Trading is a stock exchanging bunch intended to enable clients to watch and gain from an expert informal investor utilizing live screen offering to sound. We recognize, clarify, and execute live trades that our individuals can pursue and achieve from continuously. Pursue this blog to gain from star stockbrokers live in real life. Live day trading stream, day trading talk room, trade alarms, day by day online courses, and FREE video exercises.

Around one post for each month.

Since Jul 2016

5. Daytrading - Google News

Mountain View, CA

About Blog; Comprehensive forward-thinking inclusion for day trading, amassed from news sources everywhere throughout the world by Google News. Pursue google news to get the most recent report on day trading.

Around 84 posts every week.

6. Daytrading - Reddit

San Francisco, CA

About Blog Information for your ordinary dealer. We made a dissension visit to help associate you with individual informal investors. Pursue this Reddit to get articles on day trading.

Around 84 posts for each week.

7. Day Trade Review

Plano, Texas

About Blog; Day Trade Review offers exhortation and surveys to help informal investors pick the best exchanging visit rooms, specialists, and stages. Pursue this site to get news and data on Broker, Newsletter, and Financial Reviews.

Around two posts every week.

Since Mar 2017

8. Jigsaw Trading

Jigsaw Trading. About Blog; The Rated Financial Trading Software Product. Choice helps to program for expert and informal retail investors. Pursue our blog to increase an extra edge in your free day trading.

Around three posts every month.

Since Jan 2013

9. Day Trade The World

About Blog; Day Trading Stocks, Forex, Futures. Day Trade The World is a final day trading, stock trading, and prospects are trading site. Pursue this blog and figure out how to open your day trading office and upgrade your abilities.

Around two posts every week.

Since Feb 2017

10. Magic Day Trading

About Blog; MOJO Day Trading gives the training and instruments fundamental for anybody to trade the securities exchange. Pursue this site and get each data you have to think about day trading.

Around two posts for each week.

Since Sep 2014

10.   Day Trading Simulator Learn How to Trade

Washington, D.C.

About Blog; TradingSim quickens the lofty expectation to absorb information of turning into a reliably beneficial merchant by enabling you to replay the market as though you were trading live today, for any day from the most recent two years it's genuinely an trading time machine. Practice day trading or swing trading with more than 11,000 Nasdaq, NYSE, and AMEX stocks without taking a chance with your shirt? Learn with the best stock test system on the web.

Around one post for each week.

12. Day Trade To Win Blog Price Action Trading methods with Results

Boca Raton, Florida

About Blog; Trading E-small scale S&P Futures, Currencies, and Stocks. Figure out how to day trade the E-scaled down S&P and different markets with our day trading courses, trading programming, and training programs.

Around two posts for every month.

Since Feb 2009

13. Day Trading Forex Live

Michigan

About Blog; Day Trading Forex Live was established by the two brokers, Sterling and Chad, with the point of illuminating dealers about the forex market and its inside operations. Through this site, you will get familiar with specific systems and increase explicit information that will fill in as your optimal establishment in forex trading and help you how to trade well.

Around one post for each month.

14. Air conditioning Investor Blog

About Blog; AC Investor Blog by Antonio Costa. Looking to give free day trading procedures dependent on Technical Analysis.

Around one post for each week.

Since Oct 2005

15. Samurai Trading Academy

About Blog; Elite Day Trading Education and Training. Samurai Trading Academy is committed to making proficient Emini informal investors through first-class instruction and our versatile trading approach.

around one post for every month.

Since Mar 2013

16. The Mind of a Day Trader

About Blog; The Mind of a Day Trader

Around one post for every month.

Since Aug 2015

17. Securities exchange Analysis

Southeast Pennsylvania

About Blog; This Stock Blog gives an understanding on day by day financial exchange trading just as stock trading investigation. We likewise list stocks to purchase, top stocks, stock picks, and the best stocks to put resources into 2018. If you're searching for a stock blog about hot stocks that are rising, you found the perfect spot.

Around 17 posts for each week.

Since Jul 2008

18. SEE JANE TRADE

Full-Time Mom, Part Time Day merchant. A homemaker that has figured out how to day trade and make six-figure pay while being home for her family.

Around three posts every week.

Since Jan 2017

19. Cash Maker Edge - Day Trading Course

Money Maker, Edge Day Trading Course, figure out how to exchange Futures, stocks and deal with a heap of gold and silver with hazard the board and methodology.

around one post for every month.

Since Oct 2008

20. Informal investor Wayne

Day Trading Stocks For A Living. Helping YOU become a reliably profitable Day Trader.

around one post for each month.

Since Sep 2016

21. orderflowtrading.de

Germany

About Blog; The name of our site justifies itself with real evidence - 'request stream exchanging.' There is a valid justification behind this name. We are sure that the capacity to work with a request stream is significant. We will talk about the essentials of the subject in this article. Maybe, this data is outstanding for certain readers.

around one post for each week.

22. Informal investors FX

Los Angeles

About Blog; Forex Trading. DayTraders FX is home to a lively and global trading network. We center around money related markets, explicitly Foreign Exchange (Forex), and kill the brute through a part determined network with administrations including live examination, exchange alarms, private guidance, instructive classes, and significantly more.

around one post for each month.

Since Aug 2008

23. Ratgebergeld.at - Day Trading and Swing Trading

exchanging methodologies with live talk and continuous preparing

around 13 posts for every week.

Since Aug 2016

Additionally in Swing Trading web journals

24. Start-Day-Trading.com - Day Trading Blog

Start-Day-Trading.com - Day Trading BlogAbout Blog Day exchanging blog. Discourse includes day exchanging stocks, Forex, day exchanging misfortunes, day trading tips, and day trading professionally.

Recurrence around two posts for every month.

Since Jan 2017

25. Vancity Trader

Vancity TraderAbout Blog Futures Day Trading Mentorship. Learn 1 on 1 with a Professional. Take in with a Funded Trader from TopstepTrader.

around one post for every month.

Since May 2013

Additionally in Futures Trading Blogs

26. Emini Methods

Los Angeles

About Blog; for the most part about day trading e-small scale fates. A hypothetical physicist and cosmologist via preparing, e-small fates informal investor by occupation, proprietor, and website admin of eminimethods.com.

Recurrence around one post for every month.

Since Mar 2005

27. DayTrading.Buzz

New York

About Blog; Combining quick look into with innovation, our group is continually distinguishing the top potential day trading openings all through each trading day.

Recurrence around one post for each month.

Since May 2016

28. How I Day Trade

About Blog; Shorten your expectation to absorb information and learn easy to pursue day trading arrangements planned for hitting predictable singles and the occasional grand slam.

Recurrence around four posts for each week.

Since Jun 2007

29. Bear Bull Traders - Daily Trading

Vancouver, British Columbia

About Blog; Learning Community of Serious Traders. I learned it the most challenging way possible. Be that as it may, you don't need to. I share how you also can assume responsibility for your life and have success in day trading on the securities exchange. You need the correct devices, and you should be inspired, buckle down, and endure. If you do, you also can be an active informal investor.

Recurrence around one post for every month.

Since Aug 2017

30. Day Trade Arcade

Gdynia, Polska

About Blog; A Journey Beyond Day Trading. It's always about the voyage, isn't that so? That is the reason I made DayTradeArcade - to help different values informal investors share my technique about how to be productive. Visit my blog for instructive materials and methodology tips.

Recurrence around one post for every month.

Since Jul 2016

31. Day Trading Course

US

About Blog; Those who need to taste achievement in the unpredictability of day trading market are unquestionably required to upgrade their skills. For this explanation, great Day Trading, instructional classes give incredible help. It arms you with a reliable and presumed method for expanding your aptitudes and execution levels in the unpredictable and multifaceted nature of the dynamic trading market.

Around two posts for each month.

32. ForteTrader

About Blog; Day Trading Academy. We are a network of brokers that have, for the most part, similar objectives throughout everyday life, less pressure, and time opportunity.

Around one post for each month.

Since Dec 2016

33. Full Time Day Trader

About Blog; Learn how to day exchange stocks. A great many backtest outlines sponsor the Full-Time Day Trader technique; it removes the mystery from trading.

Around two posts for each week.

34. Market Dancer - One Trade at once

One Trade at a time. Day Trading Education. HOW MIGHT YOU LEARN TO BE A SUCCESSFUL DAY TRADER? THERE IS AN EASY ANSWER TO THAT. Gain from other 'Effective' Day Traders! That way you don't need to commit the errors they did. You realize that in Day Trading, the odds are not suitable for the uneducated, transient wannabees!

Recurrence around one post for every month.

Since Mar 2017

35. Renko Trading - Day trading with Renko Charts

Renko Trading - Day trading with Renko ChartsAbout Blog Renko trading blog about day trading with Renko Charts. Renkotraders.com is a site that is committed to bestowing data and information about trading with Renko diagrams. Here, you can discover all that you needed to find out about Renko outlines, including the real nuts and bolts of Renko trading to cutting edge Renko trading techniques and specialized investigation. around one post for every month.

36. Day Trading SPY

Wild ox, New York

About Blog; Day Trade SPY shows you how to day exchange SPY choices as give a pick of the day for benefits of 5% or more. We show you how to day exchange SPY alternatives to win 5% every day, utilizing our basic strategy. No spreads.

around one post for each week.

Since Feb 2014

37. The Trader Chick

About Blog; CEO Marina Kuperman Villatoro, The Trader Chick. been day exchanging the Futures Markets for quite a long time, and the number #1 thing she says is - Day Trading has become the Greatest Teacher of My Life! Day Trading is a whole lot more than basically trading the business sectors. It's tied in with turning into the best individual you can be. Also, that can be the scariest piece, all things considered.

around 84 posts for each week.

Since Mar 2013

38. 1-2-3 Day Trade

Know-How to future trading from TradeCraze. David anticipates showing you how he moves toward the business sectors and trades professionally.

around one post for every month.

Since Mar 2012

39. ClayTrader.com

Stupendous Rapids, MI

About Blog; Become a Successful Stock Trader. Figure out how to exchange stocks utilizing specialized examination. Start Investing in the securities exchange and your future today: Specialized Chart Analysis and Live Day Trading.

Recurrence around one post for each month.

40. OddStockTrader - Day Trading and Swing Trading Education

About Blog; Live Day Trading and Swing Trading. Figure out how to day exchange with live video exercises about exchanging methodologies and how to locate the hot stocks to trade for that day — exchange online today with an edge.

Recurrence around one post for every month.

Since Aug 2012

41. Boundless Prosperity - Day Trading

Australia

About Blog; The total manual for sparing, contributing, trading, and structuring your life. The Infinite Prosperity venture was made in 2011 to lift the money related knowledge and proper strengthening of customers through a bit by bit online course.

Around one post for each month.

Since May 2012

CHAPTER 14:

DAY TRADING DO'S AND DON'T'S

While we have recently discussed a portion of the trading ruins that forex merchants should quit making in 2018, we presently need to go into some more detail about the greatest Do's and Don't's in the Forex showcase. Remember the six below to help keep you destined for success with your trading!

Trading Do's

Pursue a trading plan. We have included this as the main thing on the rundown in light of current circumstances. You need to have a definite arrangement that covers each part of your trading before you venture into the Forex world. Keep in mind that without an agreement, you are not trading, you are betting. Try not to be a card shark – have a method!

Have an agenda. An agenda is number two on the rundown (it is nearly as significant as a trading plan!). On your schedule, incorporate the trading decides that must be fulfilled before you go into a trade.

This could be things like "exchange is a similar way as the general market pattern" or "reward: risk proportion is 3:1."

Having an agenda before each new trade incredibly decreases your odds of committing silly errors.

Pursue a rigorous everyday practice. The significance of a day by day trading routine is something we have discussed previously. Trading can turn into a forlorn undertaking, and some may battle with a new situation where they have no manager to guide them consistently.

Having a daily practice set up will assist you with conquering these difficulties and put you on track for a fruitful vocation as an autonomous dealer.

Trading Don't's

Become enthusiastic. Turning out to be either angry when you lose or excessively cheerful each time you make cash isn't a formula for progress as a forex dealer. The best dealers among us are the individuals who can separate their feelings totally from their trading. It is the point at which you become enthusiastic that you commit the most exceedingly terrible errors in trading. An example is attempting to compensate for a misfortune, getting excessively forceful after a success, etc. To put it plainly, this alone prompts awful results for forex dealers. Try not to become overly energetic!

Wed an exchange. Here and there in trading, you become so persuaded that a specific trading instrument will move either up or down that you totally disregard contentions and even proof of the opposite.

For instance, don't purchase Apple shares just out of your affection for iPhones. You may cherish your phone, however, as dealers, we have to look at trading openings dispassionately to succeed.

Tune in to bits of gossip. In trading, it's fundamental that you make sure to do your very own exploration consistently. Maybe you have a companion who's great at trading and has profited, yet your circumstance will even now always be somewhat unique. You don't pursue a similar trading system and strategy, you don't have the same position size, and you may not realize the actual cost or stop-misfortune that he is utilizing.

In this way, all genuine merchants do their very own examination before every trade they enter!

CPSIA information can be obtained
at www.ICGtesting.com
Printed in the USA
BVHW090337190221
600496BV00008B/629